MW00901496

Army Doctrine Reference Publication
No. 5-0

Department of the Army
Washington, DC, 17 May 2012

The Operations Process

Contents

Distribution Restriction: Approved for public release; distribution is unlimited.

i

Figures

Tables

Preface

Army doctrine reference publication (ADRP) 5-0 augments the principles of the operations process found in Army doctrine publication (ADP) 5-0, *The Operations Process*. It provides an expanded discussion of planning, preparing, executing, and assessing operations. Together with ADP 5-0, this ADRP establishes a common frame of reference and language that commanders and staffs use for the exercise of mission command.

To comprehend the doctrine contained in ADRP 5-0, readers must first understand the foundations of unified land operations described in ADP 3-0, *Unified Land Operations*. In addition, readers must fully understand the principles of mission command described in ADP 6-0, *Mission Command*. For a detailed explanation of the tactics, techniques, and procedures associated with the operations process, see Army Tactics, Techniques, and Procedures (ATTP) 5-0.1, *Commander and Staff Officer Guide*.

The principal audience for ADRP 5-0 includes Army commanders, leaders, and unit staffs (officers, noncommissioned officers, and Soldiers). Commanders and staffs of Army headquarters serving as joint task force or multinational headquarters should also refer to applicable joint or multinational doctrine concerning the range of military operations as well as joint or multinational forces. Trainers and educators throughout the Army will also use this manual.

Commanders, staffs, and subordinates ensure their decisions and actions comply with applicable U.S., international, and, in some cases, host nation laws and regulations. Commanders at all levels ensure their Soldiers operate in accordance with the law of war and the rules of engagement. (See Field Manual [FM] 27-10.)

ADRP 5-0 uses joint terms where applicable. Selected joint and Army terms and definitions appear in both the glossary and the text. Terms for which ADRP 5-0 is the proponent publication (the authority) are marked with an asterisk (*) in the glossary. Definitions for which ADRP 5-0 is the proponent publication are in boldfaced text. These terms and their definitions will be in the next revision of FM 1-02. For other definitions shown in the text, the term is italicized and the number of the proponent publication follows the definition.

ADRP 5-0 applies to the Active Army, the Army National Guard/Army National Guard of the United States, and the United States Army Reserve unless otherwise stated.

The proponent of ADRP 5-0 is the United States Army Combined Arms Center. The preparing agency is the Combined Arms Doctrine Directorate, United States Army Combined Arms Center. Send comments and recommendations on a DA Form 2028 (Recommended Changes to Publications and Blank Forms) to Commander, U.S. Army Combined Arms Center and Fort Leavenworth, ATTN: ATZL-MCK-D (ADRP 5-0), 300 McPherson Avenue, Fort Leavenworth, KS 66027-2337; by e-mail to usarmy.leavenworth.mccoe.mbx.cadd-org-mailbox@mail mil; or submit an electronic DA Form 2028.

Acknowledgement

Cover photo courtesy of the U.S. Army at
http://www.flickr.com/photos/soldiersmediacenter/6846045865/

Introduction

ADRP 5-0 is a new publication that expands on the principles of the operations process found in ADP 5-0. Overall, the doctrine in ADRP 5-0 remains consistent with Field Manual (FM) 5-0, *The Operations Process*. The most significant change from FM 5-0 is the restructuring of doctrinal information. The principles of the operations process are now found in ADP 5-0 and ADRP 5-0. A new field manual (currently under development) will address the specific tactics and procedures associated with planning, preparing, executing, and assessing operations. In the interim, ATTP 5-0.1, *Commander and Staff Officers Guide*, contains these details.

ADRP 5-0 updates doctrine on the operations process to include incorporating the Army's operational concept of unified land operations found in ADP 3-0 and the principles of mission command found in ADP 6-0. While the major activities of the operations process have not changed, the following is a summary of changes by chapter.

Chapter 1 describes the nature of operations in which commanders, supported by their staffs, exercise mission command. Next, this chapter defines and describes the operations process. A discussion of the principles commanders and staffs consider for the effective execution of the operations process follows. The chapter concludes with discussions of the integrating processes, continuing activities, battle rhythm, and running estimates. The following are significant changes from FM 5-0 in chapter 1. The principles of the operations process now include—

- Commanders drive the operations process.
- Build and maintain situational understanding.
- Apply critical and creative thinking.
- Encourage collaboration and dialogue.

ADRP 5-0 adopts the joint definitions of *operational approach*, *commander's intent*, and *risk management*. ADRP 5-0 replaces the continuing activity of *intelligence, surveillance, and reconnaissance* with *information collection*.

Chapter 2 defines planning and plans and lists the values of effective planning. Next, this chapter describes integrated planning and operational art. The chapter next describes the Army's planning methodologies: Army design methodology, the military decisionmaking process, and troop leading procedures. This chapter then describes key components of a plan or order. This chapter concludes by offering guidelines for effective planning and describes planning pitfalls that commanders and staffs guard against. The following are significant changes from FM 5-0. ADRP 5-0—

- Retitles *design* to *Army design methodology* and modifies the definition.
- Associates the Army design methodology with conceptual planning and operational art.
- Modifies the definition of the *military decisionmaking process*.
- Modifies step 7 of the military decisionmaking process from "orders production" to "orders production, dissemination, and transition."
- Reintroduces "key tasks" as a component of commander's intent.
- Modifies guidelines to effective planning.

Chapter 3 defines preparation and lists the preparation activities commonly performed within the headquarters and across the force to improve the unit's ability to execute operations. The chapter concludes by providing guidelines for effective preparation. The following are significant changes from FM 5-0. ADRP 5-0—

- Adds the preparation activity "initiate network preparations."
- Modifies the preparation activity "initiate reconnaissance and surveillance" to "initiate information collection."
- Modifies the guidelines to effective preparation.

Chapter 4 provides guidelines for effective execution. It describes the role of the commander and staff in directing and controlling current operations. Next, this chapter describes decisionmaking in execution. The chapter concludes with a discussion of the rapid decisionmaking and synchronization process. ADRP 5-0 modifies guidelines to effective execution to seize the initiative through action and accept prudent risk to exploit opportunities.

Chapter 5 defines assessment as a continuous activity of the operations process and describes its purpose. Next, it describes an assessment process and offers guidelines commanders and staffs consider for effective assessment. This chapter concludes with a discussion of assessment working groups and assessment support from operations research and systems analysis. The following are significant changes from FM 5-0. ADRP 5-0—

- Adopts the joint definition of *assessment*.
- Modifies guidelines to effective assessment.

The following appendixes formally found in FM 5-0 are now found in ATTP 5-0.1:

- Command post organization and operations.
- Military decisionmaking process.
- Troop leading procedures.
- Army operation plan and order format.
- Task organization formats.
- Running estimates.
- Formal assessment plans.
- Rehearsals.
- Military briefings.

ADRP 5-0 provides a starting point for conducting the operations process. It establishes a common frame of reference and offers intellectual tools Army leaders use to plan, prepare for, execute, and assess operations. By establishing a common approach and language for exercising mission command, doctrine promotes mutual understanding and enhances effectiveness during operations. The doctrine in this publication is a guide for action rather than a set of fixed rules. In operations, effective leaders recognize when and where doctrine, training, or even their experience no longer fits the situation, and adapt accordingly.

ADP 5-0 and ADRP 5-0 add or modify the terms listed in introductory tables 1 and 2.

Introductory Table-1. New Army terms

Term	Remarks
Army design methodology	Replaces *design*.

Introductory Table-2. Modified Army terms

Term	Remarks
assessment	Adopts the joint definition.
design	Formal definition replaced by *Army design methodology*.
direct support	Modifies the definition.
general support-reinforcing	Modifies the definition.
military decisionmaking process	Modifies the definition.
operational approach	Adopts the joint definition.
planning	Modifies the definition modified.

Chapter 1

Fundamentals of the Operations Process

The chapter describes the nature of operations in which commanders, supported by their staffs, exercise mission command. Next, this chapter defines and describes the operations process. A discussion of the principles commanders and staffs consider for the effective execution of the operations process follows. The chapter concludes with discussions of the integrating processes, continuing activities, battle rhythm, and running estimates.

THE NATURE OF OPERATIONS

1-1. To understand doctrine on mission command and the operations process, Soldiers must have an appreciation for the general nature of operations. Military operations are human endeavors, contests of wills characterized by continuous and mutual adaptation among all participants. In operations, Army forces face thinking and adaptive enemies, differing agendas of various actors (organizations and individuals), and changing perceptions of civilians in an operational area. As all sides take actions, each side reacts, learns, and adapts. Appreciating these relationships among human wills is essential to understanding the fundamental nature of operations.

1-2. In operations, friendly forces fiercely engage a multifaceted enemy force. Each side consists of numerous diverse and connected parts, each interdependent and adapting to changes within and between each other. In addition, an operational environment is not static. It continually evolves. This evolution results, in part, from humans interacting within an operational environment as well as from their ability to learn and adapt. The dynamic nature of an operational environment makes determining the relationship between cause and effect difficult and contributes to the uncertainty of military operations.

1-3. Uncertainty pervades operations in the form of unknowns about the enemy, the people, and the surroundings. Even the behavior of friendly forces is often uncertain because of human mistakes and the effects of stress on Soldiers. Chance and friction contribute to the uncertain nature of operations. The sudden death of a local leader that causes an eruption of violence illustrates chance. The combinations of countless factors that impinge on the conduct of operations, from broken equipment that slows movement to complicated plans that confuse subordinates, are examples of friction.

1-4. During operations leaders make decisions, develop plans, and direct actions under varying degrees of uncertainty. Commanders seek to counter the uncertainty of operations by empowering subordinates at the scene to make decisions, act, and quickly adapt to changing circumstances. As such, the philosophy of mission command guides commanders, staffs, and subordinates throughout the conduct of operations.

MISSION COMMAND

1-5. *Mission command* is the exercise of authority and direction by the commander using mission orders to enable disciplined initiative within the commander's intent to empower agile and adaptive leaders in the conduct of unified land operations (ADP 6-0). This philosophy of command fosters an environment of mutual trust and shared understanding among commanders, staffs, and subordinates. It requires a command climate in which commanders encourage subordinates to accept prudent risk and exercise disciplined initiative to seize opportunities and counter threats within the commander's intent. Through mission orders, commanders focus their orders on the purpose of the operation rather than on the details of how to perform assigned tasks. Doing this minimizes detailed control and allows subordinates the greatest possible freedom of action. Finally, when delegating authority to subordinates, commanders set the necessary conditions for success by allocating appropriate resources to subordinates based on assigned tasks.

1-6.   Mission command is also a warfighting function. The *mission command warfighting function* is the related tasks and systems that develop and integrate those activities enabling a commander to balance the art of command and the science of control in order to integrate the other warfighting functions (ADRP 3-0). Through the mission command warfighting function, commanders and staffs integrate the other warfighting functions into a coherent whole to mass the effects of combat power at the decisive place and time. (See ADRP 6-0 for a detailed discussion of mission command and the mission command warfighting function.)

THE OPERATIONS PROCESS

1-7.   The Army's framework for exercising mission command is the *operations process*—the major mission command activities performed during operations: planning, preparing, executing, and continuously assessing the operation (ADP 5-0). (See figure 1-1.) Commanders, supported by their staffs, use the operations process to drive the conceptual and detailed planning necessary to understand, visualize, and describe their operational environment; make and articulate decisions; and direct, lead, and assess military operations.

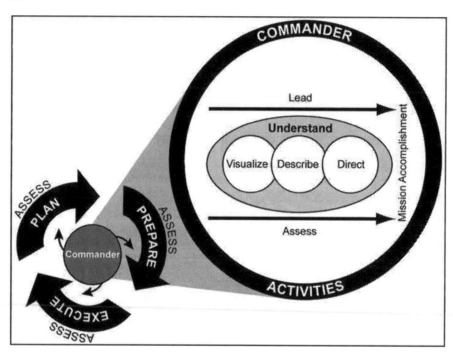

Figure 1-1. The operations process

1-8.   The activities of the operations process are not discrete; they overlap and recur as circumstances demand. Planning starts an iteration of the operations process (see chapter 2). Upon completion of the initial order, planning continues as leaders revise the plan based on changing circumstances. Preparing begins during planning and continues through execution (see chapter 3). Execution puts a plan into action by applying combat power to seize, retain, and exploit the initiative to gain a position of relative advantage (see chapter 4). Assessing is continuous and influences the other three activities (see chapter 5).

1-9.   Both the commander and staff have important roles within the operations process. The commander's role is to drive the operations process through the activities of understanding, visualizing, describing, directing, leading, and assessing operations as depicted in figure 1-1. The staff's role is to assist commanders with understanding situations, making and implementing decisions, controlling operations, and assessing progress. In addition, the staff assists subordinate units (commanders and staffs), and keeps units and organizations outside the headquarters informed throughout the conduct of operations. (See ATTP 5-0.1 for a detailed discussion of the duties and responsibilities of the staff.)

PRINCIPLES OF THE OPERATIONS PROCESS

1-10. The operations process, while simple in concept (plan, prepare, execute, and assess), is dynamic in execution. Commanders and staffs use the operations process to integrate numerous tasks executed throughout the headquarters and with subordinate units. Commanders must organize and train their staffs and subordinates as an integrated team to simultaneously plan, prepare, execute, and assess operations. In addition to the principles of mission command, commanders and staffs consider the following principles for the effective use of the operations process:

- Commanders drive the operations process.
- Build and maintain situational understanding.
- Apply critical and creative thinking.
- Encourage collaboration and dialogue.

Principles of mission command

- Build cohesive teams through mutual trust.
- Create shared understanding.
- Provide a clear commander's intent.
- Exercise disciplined initiative.
- Use mission orders.
- Accept prudent risk.

COMMANDERS DRIVE THE OPERATIONS PROCESS

1-11. Commanders are the most important participants in the operations process. While staffs perform essential functions that amplify the effectiveness of operations, commanders drive the operations process through understanding, visualizing, describing, directing, leading, and assessing operations. Accurate and timely running estimates (see paragraphs 1-68 to 1-71) are key knowledge management tools that assist commanders in driving the operations process. (See figure 1-2.)

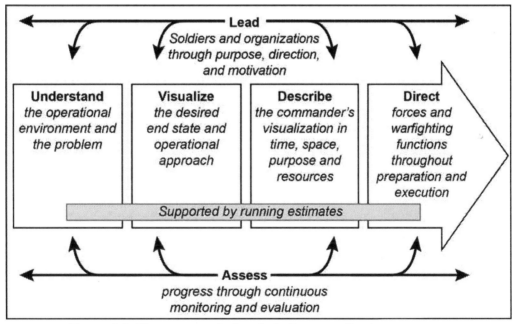

Figure 1-2. The commander's role in the operations process

Understand

1-12. Understanding is fundamental to the commander's ability to establish a situation's context. It is essential to effective decisionmaking during planning and execution. Analysis of the operational and mission variables (see paragraphs 1-32 to 1-35) provides the information used to develop understanding and frame the problem. In addition, conceptual and detailed planning assist commanders in developing their initial understanding of the operational environment and the problem (see chapter 2). To develop a better understanding of an operational environment, commanders circulate within the area of operations as often as possible, collaborating with subordinate commanders and with Soldiers. Using personal observations and inputs from others (to include running estimates from the staff), commanders improve their understanding of their operational environment throughout the operations process.

1-13. Information collection (to include reconnaissance and surveillance) is indispensable to building and improving the commander's understanding. Formulating commander's critical information requirements (CCIRs), keeping them current, determining where to place key personnel, and arranging for liaison also contribute to improving the commander's understanding. Greater understanding enables commanders to make better decisions throughout the conduct of operations.

Visualize

1-14. As commanders begin to understand their operational environment and the problem, they start visualizing a desired end state and potential solutions to solve the problem. Collectively, this is known as *commander's visualization*—the mental process of developing situational understanding, determining a desired end state, and envisioning an operational approach by which the force will achieve that end state (ADP 5-0). Assignment of a mission provides the focus for developing the commander's visualization that, in turn, provides the basis for developing plans and orders. During preparation and execution, the commander's visualization helps commanders determine if, when, and what to decide, as they adapt to changing conditions.

1-15. In building their visualization, commanders first seek to understand those conditions that represent the current situation. Next, commanders envision a set of desired future conditions that represents the operation's end state. Commanders complete their visualization by conceptualizing an *operational approach*—a description of the broad actions the force must take to transform current conditions into those desired at end state (JP 5-0). (See figure 1-3.)

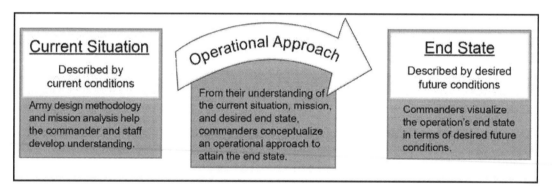

Figure 1-3. Completed commander's visualization

1-16. Commanders apply the Army design methodology and use the elements of operational art (see ADRP 3-0) when developing and describing their commander's visualization. They also actively collaborate with higher, subordinate and adjacent commanders, the staff, and unified action partners to assist them in building their visualization. *Unified action partners* are those military forces, governmental and nongovernmental organizations, and elements of the private sector with whom Army forces plan, coordinate, synchronize, and integrate during the conduct of operations (ADRP 3-0). Because of the dynamic nature of military operations, commanders must continuously validate their visualization throughout the operations process.

Describe

1-17. After commanders visualize an operation, they describe it to their staffs and subordinates to facilitate shared understanding and purpose. During planning, commanders ensure subordinates understand their visualization well enough to begin course of action development. During execution, commanders describe modifications to their visualization in updated planning guidance and directives resulting in fragmentary orders that adjust the original order. Commanders describe their visualization in doctrinal terms, refining and clarifying it, as circumstances require. Commanders express their visualization in terms of—

- Commander's intent.
- Planning guidance, including an operational approach.
- Commander's critical information requirements.
- Essential elements of friendly information.

Commander's Intent

1-18. The *commander's intent* is a clear and concise expression of the purpose of the operation and the desired military end state that supports mission command, provides focus to the staff, and helps subordinate and supporting commanders act to achieve the commander's desired results without further orders, even when the operation does not unfold as planned (JP 3-0). During planning, the initial commander's intent drives course of action development. In execution, the commander's intent guides disciplined initiative as subordinates make decisions when facing unforeseen opportunities or countering threats.

1-19. Commanders develop their intent statement personally. It must be easy to remember and clearly understood by commanders and staffs two echelons lower in the chain of command. The more concise the commander's intent, the easier it is to recall and understand. (See chapter 2 for a discussion of writing the commander's intent statement.)

Planning Guidance

1-20. Commanders provide planning guidance to the staff based upon their visualization. Planning guidance must convey the essence of the commander's visualization, including a description of the operational approach. Effective planning guidance reflects how the commander sees the operation unfolding. It broadly describes when, where, and how the commander intends to employ combat power to accomplish the mission, within the higher commander's intent. Broad and general guidance gives the staff and subordinate leaders' maximum latitude; it lets proficient staffs develop flexible and effective options.

1-21. Commanders use their experience and judgment to add depth and clarity to their planning guidance. They ensure staffs understand the broad outline of their visualization while allowing them the latitude necessary to explore different options. This guidance provides the basis for the concept of operations without dictating the specifics of the final plan. As with their intent, commanders may modify planning guidance based on staff and subordinate input and changing conditions. (See ATTP 5-0.1 for a detailed discussion of developing and issue planning guidance.)

Commander's Critical Information Requirements

1-22. A *commander's critical information requirement* is an information requirement identified by the commander as being critical to facilitating timely decisionmaking. The two key elements are friendly force information requirements and priority intelligence requirements (JP 3-0). A commander's critical information requirement (CCIR) directly influences decisionmaking and facilitates the successful execution of military operations. Commanders decide to designate an information requirement as a CCIR based on likely decisions and their visualization of the course of the operation. A CCIR may support one or more decisions. During planning, staffs recommend information requirements for commanders to designate as CCIRs. During preparation and execution, they recommend changes to CCIRs based on assessment. A CCIR is—

- Specified by a commander for a specific operation.
- Applicable only to the commander who specifies it.
- Situation dependent—directly linked to a current or future mission.
- Time-sensitive.

1-23. Always promulgated by a plan or order, commanders limit the number of CCIRs to focus the efforts of limited collection assets. The fewer the CCIRs, the easier it is for staffs to remember, recognize, and act on each one. This helps staffs and subordinates identify information the commander needs immediately. While most staffs provide relevant information, a good staff expertly distills that information. It identifies answers to CCIRs and gets them to the commander immediately. It also identifies vital information that does not answer a CCIR but that the commander nonetheless needs to know. A good staff develops this ability through training and experience. Designating too many CCIRs limits the staff's ability to immediately recognize and react to them. Excessive critical items reduce the focus of collection efforts.

1-24. The list of CCIRs constantly changes. Commanders add and delete them throughout an operation based on the information needed for specific decisions. Commanders determine their own CCIRs, but they may select some from staff nominations. Once approved, a CCIR falls into one of two categories: priority intelligence requirements (PIRs) and friendly force information requirements (FFIRs).

1-25. A *priority intelligence requirement* is an intelligence requirement, stated as a priority for intelligence support, that the commander and staff need to understand the adversary or the operational environment (JP 2-0). PIRs identify the information about the enemy and other aspects of the operational environment that the commander considers most important. Lessons from recent operations show that intelligence about civil considerations may be as critical as intelligence about the enemy. Thus, all staff sections may recommend information about civil considerations as PIRs. The intelligence officer manages PIRs for the commander through planning requirements and assessing collection.

1-26. A *friendly force information requirement* is information the commander and staff need to understand the status of friendly force and supporting capabilities (JP 3-0). FFIRs identify the information about the mission, troops and support available, and time available for friendly forces that the commander considers most important. In coordination with the staff, the operations officer manages FFIRs for the commander.

Essential Elements of Friendly Information

1-27. Commanders also describe information they want protected as essential elements of friendly information. An ***essential element of friendly information* is a critical aspect of a friendly operation that, if known by the enemy, would subsequently compromise, lead to failure, or limit success of the operation and therefore should be protected from enemy detection**. Although EEFIs are not CCIRs, they have the same priority. EEFIs establish elements of information to protect rather than ones to collect. Their identification is the first step in the operations security process and central to the protection of information.

Direct

1-28. Commanders direct all aspects of operations by establishing their commander's intent, setting achievable objectives, and issuing clear tasks to subordinate units. Throughout the operations process, commanders direct forces by—

- Preparing and approving plans and orders.
- Establishing command and support relationships.
- Assigning and adjusting tasks, control measures, and task organization.
- Positioning units to maximize combat power.
- Positioning key leaders at critical places and times to ensure supervision.
- Allocating resources to exploit opportunities and counter threats.
- Committing the reserve as required.

Lead

1-29. Through leadership, commanders provide purpose, direction, and motivation to subordinate commanders, their staff, and Soldiers. In many instances, a commander's physical presence is necessary to lead effectively. Where the commander locates within the area of operations is an important leadership consideration. Commanders balance their time between leading the staff through the operations process and providing purpose, direction, and motivation to subordinate commanders and Soldiers away from the command post.

Assess

1-30. Commanders continuously assess the situation to better understand current conditions and determine how the operation is progressing. Continuous assessment helps commanders anticipate and adapt the force to changing circumstances. Commanders incorporate the assessments of the staff, subordinate commanders, and unified action partners into their personal assessment of the situation. Based on their assessment, commanders modify plans and orders to adapt the force to changing circumstances.

BUILD AND MAINTAIN SITUATIONAL UNDERSTANDING

1-31. Success in operations demands timely and effective decisions based on applying judgment to available information and knowledge. As such, commanders and staffs seek to build and maintain situational understanding throughout the operations process. *Situational understanding* is the product of applying analysis and judgment to relevant information to determine the relationships among the operational and mission variables to facilitate decisionmaking (ADP 5-0). Building and maintaining situational understanding is essential to establishing the situation's context, developing effective plans, assessing operations, and making quality decisions throughout the operations process. Commanders continually strive to maintain their situational understanding and work through periods of reduced understanding as the situation evolves.

Operational and Mission Variables

1-32. Commanders and staffs use the operational and mission variables to help build their situational understanding. They analyze and describe an operational environment in terms of eight interrelated operational variables: political, military, economic, social, information, infrastructure, physical environment, and time (PMESII-PT). Upon receipt of a mission, commanders filter information categorized by the operational variables into relevant information with respect to the mission. They use the mission variables, in combination with the operational variables, to refine their understanding of the situation and to visualize, describe, and direct operations. The mission variables are mission, enemy, terrain and weather, troops and support available, time available, and civil considerations (METT-TC).

Operational Variables

1-33. The operational variables are fundamental to developing a comprehensive understanding of an operational environment. Table 1-1 provides a brief description of each variable.

Table 1-1. Operational variables

Variable	Description
Political	Describes the distribution of responsibility and power at all levels of governance—formally constituted authorities, as well as informal or covert political powers
Military	Explores the military and paramilitary capabilities of all relevant actors (enemy, friendly, and neutral) in a given operational environment
Economic	Encompasses individual and group behaviors related to producing, distributing, and consuming resources
Social	Describes the cultural, religious, and ethnic makeup within an operational environment and the beliefs, values, customs, and behaviors of society members
Information	Describes the nature, scope, characteristics, and effects of individuals, organizations, and systems that collect, process, disseminate, or act on information
Infrastructure	Is composed of the basic facilities, services, and installations needed for the functioning of a community or society
Physical environment	Includes the geography and manmade structures, as well as the climate and weather in the area of operations
Time	Describes the timing and duration of activities, events, or conditions within an operational environment, as well as how the timing and duration are perceived by various actors in the operational environment

1-34. Each of the eight operational variables also has associated subvariables. Table 1-2 lists examples of subvariables that might require consideration within each operational variable.

Table 1-2. Operational subvariables

Political variable	Social variable	Physical environment variable
Attitude toward the United States Centers of political power Type of government Government effectiveness and legitimacy Influential political groups International relationships	Demographic mix Social volatility Education level Ethnic diversity Religious diversity Population movement Common languages Criminal activity Human rights Centers of social power Basic cultural norms and values	Terrain • Observation and fields of fire • Avenues of approach • Key terrain • Obstacles • Cover and concealment • Landforms • Vegetation • Terrain complexity • Mobility classification Natural Hazards Climate
Military variable	**Information variable**	Weather
Military forces Government paramilitary forces Nonstate paramilitary forces Unarmed combatants Nonmilitary armed combatants Military functions • Command and control (mission command) • Maneuver • Information warfare • Reconnaissance, intelligence, surveillance, and target acquisition • Fire support • Protection • Logistics	Public communications media Information warfare • Electronic warfare • Computer warfare • Information attack • Deception • Physical destruction • Protection and security measures • Perception management Intelligence Information management	• Precipitation • High temperature-heat index • Low temperature-wind chill index • Wind • Visibility • Cloud cover • Relative humidity
Economic variable	**Infrastructure variable**	**Time variable**
Economic diversity Employment status Economic activity Illegal economic activity Banking and finance	Construction pattern Urban zones Urbanized building density Utilities present Utility level Transportation architecture	Cultural perception of time Information offset Tactical exploitation of time Key dates, time periods, or events

Mission Variables

1-35. Mission variables describe characteristics of the area of operations, focusing on how they might affect a mission. Incorporating the analysis of the operational variables into METT–TC ensures Army leaders consider the best available relevant information about conditions that pertain to the mission. Using the operational variables as a source of relevant information for the mission variables allows commanders to refine their situational understanding of their operational environment and to visualize, describe, direct, lead and assess operations. Table 1-3 provides a brief description of each of the mission variables.

Table 1-3. Mission variables

Variable	Description
Mission	Commanders and staffs view all of the mission variables in terms of their impact on mission accomplishment. The mission is the task, together with the purpose, that clearly indicates the action to be taken and the reason therefore. It is always the first variable commanders consider during decisionmaking. A mission statement contains the "who, what, when, where, and why" of the operation.
Enemy	The second variable to consider is the enemy—dispositions (including organization, strength, location, and tactical mobility), doctrine, equipment, capabilities, vulnerabilities, and probable courses of action.
Terrain and weather	Terrain and weather analysis are inseparable and directly influence each other's impact on military operations. Terrain includes natural features (such as rivers and mountains) and manmade features (such as cities, airfields, and bridges). Commanders analyze terrain using the five military aspects of terrain expressed in the memory aid OAKOC: observation and fields of fire, avenues of approach, key and decisive terrain, obstacles, cover and concealment. The military aspects of weather include visibility, wind, precipitation, cloud cover, temperature, humidity.
Troops and support available	This variable includes the number, type, capabilities, and condition of available friendly troops and support. These include supplies, services, and support available from joint, host nation and unified action partners. They also include support from civilians and contractors employed by military organizations, such as the Defense Logistics Agency and the Army Materiel Command.
Time available	Commanders assess the time available for planning, preparing, and executing tasks and operations. This includes the time required to assemble, deploy, and maneuver units in relationship to the enemy and conditions.
Civil considerations	*Civil considerations* **are the influence of manmade infrastructure, civilian institutions, and activities of the civilian leaders, populations, and organizations within an area of operations on the conduct of military operations.** Civil considerations comprise six characteristics, expressed in the memory aid ASCOPE: areas, structures, capabilities, organizations, people, and events.

Cultural Understanding

1-36. As part of building their situational understanding, commanders consider how culture (both their own and others within an operational area) affects operations. Culture is the shared beliefs, values, norms, customs, behaviors, and artifacts members of a society use to cope with the world and each other. Culture influences how people make judgments about what is right and wrong and how they assess what is important and unimportant. Culture provides a framework for thought and decisions. What one culture considers rational, another culture may consider irrational. Understanding the culture of a particular society or group within a society can significantly improve the force's ability to accomplish the mission.

1-37. Understanding other cultures applies to all operations, not just operations dominated by stability. Leaders are mindful of cultural factors in four contexts:

- Awareness of how one's own culture affects how one perceives a situation.
- Awareness of the cultures within a region where the unit operates.
- Awareness of how history has shaped the culture of a region where the unit operates.
- Sensitivity to the different backgrounds, traditions, and operational methods of the various unified action partners.

1-38. Effective Army leaders understand and appreciate their own culture (individual, military, and national) in relation to the various cultures of others in the operational area. Just as culture shapes how other groups view themselves and the world around them, culture shapes how commanders, leaders, and Soldiers perceive the world. Individuals tend to interpret events according to the principles and values intrinsic to their culture. Effective commanders acknowledge that their individual perceptions greatly influence how they understand situations and make decisions. Through reflection, collaboration, and analysis of differences between their culture and the cultures in the operational area, commanders expose and question their assumptions about the situation.

1-39. Understanding the culture of unified action partners is crucial to building mutual trust and shared understanding. Army leaders take the time to learn the customs as well as the doctrine and procedures of their partners. These leaders consider how culture influences the situational understanding and decisionmaking of their military and civilian partners. This mutual understanding between leaders and their counterparts helps build unity of effort.

APPLY CRITICAL AND CREATIVE THINKING

1-40. Commanders and staffs apply critical and creative thinking throughout the operations process to assist them with understanding situations, making decisions, and directing action. Critical thinking is purposeful and reflective judgment about what to believe or what to do in response to observations, experience, verbal or written expressions, or arguments. Creative thinking involves creating something new or original. Creative thinking leads to new insights, novel approaches, fresh perspectives, and new ways of understanding and conceiving things.

1-41. Critical and creative thinking are indispensible to the operations process. For both commanders and staffs, these two skills begin with a rigorous analysis of friendly and enemy forces, as they relate to one another in time and space. This analysis includes weapons systems ranges, mobility options afforded by terrain and weather, operational reach, communications systems ranges, sustainment, and other considerations of the operational and mission variables. Disciplined and focused analysis of the operational and mission variables, coupled with critical and creative thinking about the challenges and opportunities resulting from that analysis, is essential to developing a full appreciation of the range of alternatives available to accomplish missions.

1-42. Red teams assist commanders and staffs with critical and creative thinking and help them avoid groupthink, mirror imaging, cultural missteps, and tunnel vision throughout the conduct of operations. Red teaming enables commanders to explore alternative plans and operations in the context of their operational environment, and from the perspective of unified action partners, adversaries, and others. Throughout the operations process, red team members help identify relevant actors, clarify the problem, and explain how others (unified action partners, the population, and the enemy) may view the problem from their perspectives. They challenge assumptions and the analysis used to build the plan. In essence, red teams provide commanders and staffs with an independent capability to challenge the organization's thinking. (See ATTP 5-0.1 for a more detailed discussion of the duties and responsibilities of red teams assigned to divisions, corps, and Army service component commands.)

ENCOURAGE COLLABORATION AND DIALOGUE

1-43. Throughout the operations process, commanders encourage continuous collaboration and dialogue among the staff and with unified action partners. Collaboration and dialogue aids in developing shared understanding throughout the force and with unified action partners. Collaboration is two or more people or organizations working together toward common goals by sharing knowledge and building consensus. Dialogue is a way to collaborate that involves the candid exchange of ideas or opinions among participants and that encourages frank discussions in areas of disagreement. Throughout the operations process, commanders, subordinate commanders, staffs, and unified action partners actively collaborate and dialogue, sharing and questioning information, perceptions, and ideas to better understand situations and make decisions.

1-44. Through collaboration and dialogue, the commander creates a learning environment by allowing participants to think critically and creatively and share their ideas, opinions, and recommendations without fear of retribution. Effective dialogue requires candor and a free, yet mutually respectful, competition of ideas. Participants must feel free to make viewpoints based on their expertise, experience, and insight; this includes sharing ideas that contradict the opinions held by those of higher rank. Successful commanders willingly listen to novel ideas and counterarguments concerning any problem.

1-45. Collaboration occurs during planning and continues through execution regardless of the physical location of participants. Today's information systems and collaborative planning tools enable commanders and staffs worldwide to collaborate in near real time. During planning, commanders, subordinates, and partners share their understanding of the situation, participate in course of action development and decisionmaking, and resolve conflicts before the higher headquarters issues the operation order. This collaboration results in an improved understanding of the situation, commander's intent, concept of operations, and tasks to subordinate units throughout the force. Since all echelons develop their plans nearly simultaneously, collaborative planning shortens planning time.

1-46. Similar benefits of collaboration apply during preparation and execution. Commanders, subordinates, and unified action partners compare assessments of the situation and exchange ideas on how to act during execution. Coupled with firm decisionmaking by the commander, collaboration and dialogue enable the force to adapt quickly to changing conditions. Assessment, which occurs continuously, is enhanced when commanders and subordinates collaborate in assessing the progress of the operation, to include sharing ideas on what is or is not working and how to modify plans to better accomplish the mission.

INTEGRATING PROCESSES AND CONTINUING ACTIVITIES

1-47. Throughout the operations process, commanders and staffs integrate the warfighting functions to synchronize the force in accordance with the commander's intent and concept of operations. Commanders and staffs use several integrating processes and continuing activities to do this.

INTEGRATING PROCESSES

1-48. In addition to the major activities of the operations process, commanders and staffs use several integrating processes to synchronize specific functions throughout the operations process. The integrating processes are—

- Intelligence preparation of the battlefield.
- Targeting.
- Risk management.

Intelligence Preparation of the Battlefield

1-49. Intelligence preparation of the battlefield (IPB) is a systematic, continuous process of analyzing the threat and other aspects of an operational environment within a specific geographic area. Led by the intelligence officer, the entire staff participates in IPB to develop and sustain an understanding of the enemy, terrain and weather, and civil considerations. IPB helps identify options available to friendly and threat forces.

1-50. IPB consists of four steps. Each step is performed or assessed and refined to ensure that IPB products remain complete and relevant. The four IPB steps are—

- Define the operational environment.
- Describe environmental effects on operations.
- Evaluate the threat.
- Determine threat courses of action.

1-51. IPB supports all activities of the operations process. IPB identifies gaps in current intelligence. IPB products help commanders, subordinate commanders, and staffs understand the threat, physical environment, and civil considerations throughout the operations process.

Targeting

1-52. *Targeting* is the process of selecting and prioritizing targets and matching the appropriate response to them, considering operational requirements and capabilities (JP 3-0). The purpose of targeting is to integrate and synchronize fires into operations. Targeting begins in planning, and it is an iterative process that continues through preparation and execution. The steps of the Army's targeting process are—

- Decide.
- Detect.
- Deliver.
- Assess.

This methodology facilitates engagement of the right target, at the right time, with the most appropriate assets based on the commander's targeting guidance and objectives.

1-53. The chief of staff (executive officer) or the chief of fires (fire support officer) leads the staff through the targeting process. Based on the commander's guidance and priorities, the staff determines which targets to engage and how, where, and when to engage them. The staff then assigns friendly capabilities best suited to produce the desired effect on each target, while ensuring compliance with the rules of engagement.

1-54. An important part of targeting is identifying possibilities for fratricide and collateral damage. Commanders then establish the control measures necessary to minimize the chance of these events. These measures (fire support control measures, no-strike list, airspace control measures, and others) are included in the operation order.

Risk Management

1-55. *Risk management* is the process of identifying, assessing, and controlling risks arising from operational factors and making decisions that balance risk cost with mission benefits (JP 3-0). Identifying and accepting prudent risk is a principle of mission command. Throughout the operations process, commanders and staffs use risk management to identify and mitigate risks associated with all hazards that have the potential to injure or kill friendly and civilian personnel, damage or destroy equipment, or otherwise impact mission effectiveness. Like targeting, risk management begins in planning and continues through preparation and execution. Risk management consists of the following steps:

- Identify hazards.
- Assess hazards to determine risks.
- Develop controls and make risk decisions.
- Implement controls.
- Supervise and evaluate.

1-56. All staff elements incorporate risk management into their running estimates and provide recommendations for control measures to mitigate risk within their areas of expertise. Risk management integration during all operations process activities is the primary responsibility of the unit's protection officer or the operations officer.

CONTINUING ACTIVITIES

1-57. While units execute numerous tasks throughout the operations process, commanders and staffs always plan for and coordinate the following continuing activities:

- Liaison.
- Information collection.
- Security operations.
- Protection.
- Terrain management.
- Airspace control.

Liaison

1-58. *Liaison* is that contact or intercommunication maintained between elements of military forces or other agencies to ensure mutual understanding and unity of purpose and action (JP 3-08). Most commonly used for establishing and maintaining close communications, liaison continuously enables direct, physical communications between commands. Commanders use liaison during operations and normal daily activities to help facilitate communications between organizations, preserve freedom of action, and maintain flexibility. Effective liaison ensures commanders that subordinates understand implicit coordination. Liaison provides commanders with relevant information and answers to operational questions, thus enhancing the commander's situational understanding. (See ATTP 5-0.1 for a detailed discussion on liaison.)

Information Collection

1-59. *Information collection* is an activity that synchronizes and integrates the planning and employment of sensors and assets as well as the processing, exploitation, and dissemination of systems in direct support of current and future operations (FM 3-55). It integrates the functions of the intelligence and operations staffs focused on answering the commander's critical information requirements. Joint operations refer to this as intelligence, surveillance, and reconnaissance. (See FM 3-55 for a detailed discussion of information collection.)

Security Operations

1-60. Commanders and staffs continuously plan for and coordinate security operations throughout the conduct of operations. *Security operations* are those operations undertaken by a commander to provide early and accurate warning of enemy operations, to provide the force being protected with time and maneuver space within which to react to the enemy, and to develop the situation to allow the commander to effectively use the protected force (FM 3-90). The five forms of security operations are screen, guard, cover, area security, and local security. (See FM 3-90 for a detailed discussion of security operations.)

Protection

1-61. *Protection* is the preservation of the effectiveness and survivability of mission-related military and nonmilitary personnel, equipment, facilities, information, and infrastructure deployed or located within or outside the boundaries of a given operational area (JP 3-0). Commanders and staffs synchronize, integrate, and organize capabilities and resources throughout the operations process in order to preserve combat power and mitigate the effects of threats and hazards. Protection is both a warfighting function and a continuing activity of the operations process. Commanders ensure the various tasks of protection are integrated into all aspects of operations to safeguard the force, personnel (combatants and noncombatants), systems, and physical assets.

Terrain Management

1-62. **Terrain management is the process of allocating terrain by establishing areas of operation, designating assembly areas, and specifying locations for units and activities to deconflict activities that might interfere with each other.** Throughout the operations process, commanders assigned an area of operations manage terrain within their boundaries. Through terrain management, commanders identify and locate units in the area. The operations officer, with support from others in the staff, can then deconflict operations, control movements, and deter fratricide as units get in position to execute planned missions. Commanders also consider unified action partners located in their area of operations and coordinate with them for the use of terrain.

Airspace Control

1-63. *Airspace control* is the process used to increase operational effectiveness by promoting the safe, efficient, and flexible use of airspace (JP 3-52).Throughout the operations process, commanders and staffs must integrate and synchronize forces and warfighting functions within an area of operations (ground and air). Through airspace control, commanders and staffs establish both positive and procedural controls to maximize the use of airspace to facilitate air-ground operations.

1-64. Airspace is inherently joint, and the Army processes and systems used to control and manage airspace are joint compliant. The Army's system for airspace control is the Army air-ground system. The Army air-ground system helps commanders and staffs integrate and synchronize Army airspace users with other unified action partner airspace users.

BATTLE RHYTHM

1-65. Within the operations process, commanders and staffs must integrate and synchronize numerous activities, meetings, and reports within their headquarters, with their higher headquarters, and with subordinate units. They do this by establishing the unit's battle rhythm. *Battle rhythm* is a deliberate daily cycle of command, staff, and unit activities intended to synchronize current and future operations (JP 3-33). The unit's battle rhythm sequences the actions and events within a headquarters that are regulated by the flow and sharing of information that supports decisionmaking. An effective battle rhythm—

- Establishes a routine for staff interaction and coordination.
- Facilitates interaction between the commander, staff, and subordinate units.
- Facilitates planning by the staff and decisionmaking by the commander.

1-66. As a practical matter, a headquarters' battle rhythm consists of a series of meetings, report requirements, and other activities synchronized by time and purpose. These activities may be daily, weekly, monthly, or quarterly depending on the planning horizon. **A *planning horizon* is a point in time commanders use to focus the organization's planning efforts to shape future events.** The planning horizons are short, mid, and long and correspond to the integrating cells within a headquarters: current operations cell, future operations cell, and plans cell.

1-67. Commanders adjust the unit's battle rhythm as operations progress. For example, early in the operation a commander may require a daily plans update briefing. As the situation changes, the commander may only require a plans update briefing once a week. Some factors that help determine a unit's battle rhythm include the staff's proficiency, higher headquarters' battle rhythm, and current mission. In developing the unit's battle rhythm, commanders and the chief of staff or executive officer consider—

- Higher headquarters' battle rhythm and report requirements.
- The duration and intensity of the operation.
- Planning requirements of the integrating cells (current operations, future operations, and plans).

1-68. Meetings (including working groups and boards) take up a large amount of a unit's battle rhythm. Meetings are gatherings to present and exchange information, solve problems, coordinate action, and make decisions. They may involve the staff; the commander and staff; or the commander, subordinate commanders, staff, and other partners. Who attends depends on the issue. Commanders establish meetings to integrate the staff and enhance planning and decisionmaking within the headquarters. Commanders also identify staff members to participate in the higher commander's meetings. (See ATTP 5-0.1 for a discussion of command post operations to include establishing working groups and boards. See JP 3-33 for a discussion of the various working groups and boards used by joint force commanders.)

RUNNING ESTIMATES

1-69. Effective plans and successful execution hinge on accurate and current running estimates. A *running estimate* is the continuous assessment of the current situation used to determine if the current operation is proceeding according to the commander's intent and if planned future operations are supportable (ADP 5-0). Failure to maintain accurate running estimates may lead to errors or omissions that result in flawed plans or bad decisions during execution.

1-70. Running estimates are principal knowledge management tools used by the commander and staff throughout the operations process. In their running estimates, the commander and each staff section continuously consider the effect of new information and update the following:

- Facts.
- Assumptions.
- Friendly force status.
- Enemy activities and capabilities.
- Civil considerations.
- Conclusions and recommendations.

1-71. Running estimates always include recommendations for anticipated decisions. During planning, commanders use these recommendations to select feasible, acceptable, and suitable courses of action for further analysis. During preparation and execution, commanders use recommendations from running estimates in decisionmaking.

1-72. While staffs maintain formal running estimates, the commander's estimate is a mental process directly tied to the commander's visualization. Commanders integrate personal knowledge of the situation, analysis of the operational and mission variables, assessments by subordinate commanders and other organizations, and relevant details gained from running estimates. Commanders use their running estimates to crosscheck and supplement the running estimates of the staff. (See ATTP 5-0.1 for running estimate formats).

Chapter 2

Planning

This chapter begins by defining planning and plans and lists the value of effective planning. This chapter then describes integrated planning and operational art. The chapter next describes the Army's planning methodologies: Army design methodology, the military decisionmaking process, and troop leading procedures. This chapter then describes key components of a plan or order. This chapter concludes by offering guides for effective planning and describes planning pitfalls that commanders and staffs guard against. (See JP 5-0 for doctrine on joint operations and campaign planning.)

PLANNING AND PLANS

2-1. *Planning* is the art and science of understanding a situation, envisioning a desired future, and laying out effective ways of bringing that future about (ADP 5-0). Planning helps commanders create and communicate a common vision between commanders, their staffs, subordinate commanders, and unified action partners. Planning results in a plan and orders that synchronize the action of forces in time, space, and purpose to achieve objectives and accomplish missions.

2-2. Planning is both a continuous and a cyclical activity of the operations process. While planning may start an iteration of the operations process, planning does not stop with the production of an order. During preparation and execution, the plan is continuously refined as the situation changes. Through assessment, subordinates and others provide feedback as to what is working, what is not working, and how the force can do things better. In some circumstances, commanders may determine that the current order (to include associated branches and sequels) is no longer relevant to the situation. In these instances, instead of modifying the current plan, commanders reframe the problem and develop an entirely new plan.

2-3. Planning may be highly structured, involving the commander, staff, subordinate commanders, and others to develop a fully synchronized plan or order. Planning may also be less structured, involving a platoon leader and squad leaders rapidly determining a scheme of maneuver for a hasty attack. Planning is conducted for different planning horizons, from long-range to short-range. Depending on the echelon and circumstances, units may plan in years, months, or weeks, or in days, hours, and minutes.

2-4. A product of planning is a plan or order—a directive for future action. Commanders issue plans and orders to subordinates to communicate their understanding of the situation and their visualization of an operation. A plan is a continuous, evolving framework of anticipated actions that maximizes opportunities. It guides subordinates as they progress through each phase of the operation. Any plan or order is a framework from which to adapt, not a script to be followed to the letter. The measure of a good plan is not whether execution transpires as planned, but whether the plan facilitates effective action in the face of unforeseen events. Good plans and orders foster initiative.

2-5. Plans and orders come in many forms and vary in the scope, complexity, and length of time they address. Generally, commanders and staffs develop a plan well in advance of execution, and the plan is not executed until directed. A plan becomes an order when directed for execution based on a specific time or event. Some planning results in written orders complete with attachments. Other planning produces brief fragmentary orders first issued verbally and then followed in writing.

THE VALUE OF PLANNING

2-6. All planning is based on imperfect knowledge and assumptions about the future. Planning cannot predict exactly what the effects of the operation will be, how enemies will behave with precision, or how civilians will respond to the friendly force or the enemy. Nonetheless, the understanding and learning that occurs during planning have great value. Even if units do not execute the plan precisely as envisioned—and few ever do—the process of planning results in improved situational understanding that facilitates future decisionmaking. General of the Army Dwight D. Eisenhower referred to this quality of planning when saying, "In preparing for battle I have always found that plans are useless, but planning is indispensable."

2-7.   All military activities benefit from some kind of planning. If commanders had no way to influence the future, if they believed that the natural course of events would lead to a satisfactory outcome, or if they could achieve the desired results purely by reacting, they would have no reason to plan. While there may be instances where these conditions apply, they are rare. Planning and plans help leaders—

*   Understand and develop solutions to problems.
*   Anticipate events and adapt to changing circumstances.
*   Task-organize the force and prioritize efforts.

UNDERSTAND AND DEVELOP SOLUTIONS TO PROBLEMS

2-8.   A problem is an issue or obstacle that makes it difficult to achieve a desired goal or objective. In a broad sense, a problem exists when an individual becomes aware of a significant difference between what actually is and what is desired. In the context of operations, an operational problem is the issue or set of issues that impede commanders from achieving their desired end state.

2-9.   Throughout operations, Army leaders face various problems, often requiring unique and creative solutions. Planning helps commanders and staffs understand problems and develop solutions. Not all problems require the same level of planning. For simple problems, leaders often identify them and quickly decide on a solution—sometimes on the spot. Planning is critical, however, when a problem is actually a set of interrelated issues, and the solution to each affects the others. For unfamiliar situations, planning offers ways to deal with the complete set of problems as a whole. In general, the more complex a situation is, the more important and involved the planning effort becomes.

2-10. Just as planning is only part of the operations process, planning is only part of problem solving. In addition to planning, problem solving includes implementing the planned solution (execution), learning from the implementation of the solution (assessment), and modifying or developing a new solution as required. The object of problem solving is not just to solve near-term problems, but to do so in a way that forms the basis for long-term success.

ANTICIPATE EVENTS AND ADAPT TO CHANGING CIRCUMSTANCES

2-11. The defining challenges to effective planning are uncertainty and time. Uncertainty increases with the length of the planning horizon and the rate of change in an operational environment. A tension exists between the desire to plan far into the future to facilitate preparation and the fact that the farther into the future the commander plans, the less certain the plan will remain relevant. Given the uncertain nature of operations, the object of planning is not to eliminate uncertainty, but to develop a framework for action in the midst of such uncertainty.

2-12. Planning provides an informed forecast of how future events may unfold. It entails identifying and evaluating potential decisions and actions in advance to include thinking through consequences of certain actions. Planning involves thinking about ways to influence the future as well as how to respond to potential events. Put simply, planning is thinking critically and creatively about what to do and how to do it, while anticipating changes along the way.

2-13. Planning keeps the force oriented on future objectives despite the requirements of current operations. By anticipating events beforehand, planning helps the force seize, retain, or exploit the initiative. As a result, the force anticipates events and acts purposefully and effectively before the enemy can act or before situations deteriorate. In addition, planning helps anticipate favorable turns of events that could be exploited. For example, commanders may develop a branch plan for a pursuit in the event enemy resistance is less than expected. Identifying decision points and developing branch plans and sequels associated with those decision points is a key to effective planning.

TASK-ORGANIZE THE FORCE AND PRIORITIZE EFFORTS

2-14. A key aspect of planning is organizing the force for operations. *Task-organizing* is the act of configuring an operating force, support staff, or sustainment package of specific size and composition to meet a unique task or mission (ADRP 3-0). Through task organization, commanders establish command or support relationships and allocate resources to weight the decisive operation or main effort. Command and support relationships provide the basis for unity of command and unity of effort in operations. (See paragraphs 2-75 to 2-90 for a discussion of Army command and support relationships.)

2-15. In addition to task-organizing, commanders establish priorities of support. A *priority of support* is a **priority set by the commander to ensure a subordinate unit has support in accordance with its relative importance to accomplish the mission.** Priorities of movement, fires, sustainment, protection, and information all illustrate priorities of support that commanders use to weight the decisive operation, or the main effort in phased operations.

2-16. The concept of operations may also identify a main effort (if required); otherwise, the priorities of support go to the unit conducting the decisive operation. The *main effort* is a designated subordinate unit whose mission at a given point in time is most critical to overall mission success (ADRP 3-0). It is usually weighted with the preponderance of combat power. Designating a main effort temporarily gives that unit priority of support. Commanders shift resources and priorities to the main effort as circumstances and the commander's intent require. Commanders may shift the main effort several times during an operation.

INTEGRATING PLANNING

2-17. Planning activities occupy a continuum ranging from conceptual to detailed (see figure 2-1). On one end of the continuum is conceptual planning. Understanding the operational environment and the problem, determining the operation's end state, establishing objectives, and sequencing the operation in broad terms all illustrate conceptual planning. Conceptual planning generally corresponds to the art of operations and is the focus of the commander with staff support. The commander's activities of understanding and visualization (see chapter 1) are key aspects of conceptual planning.

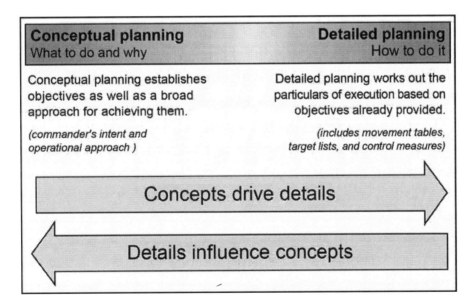

Figure 2-1. Integrated planning

2-18. At the other end of the continuum is detailed planning. Detailed planning translates the broad operational approach into a complete and practical plan. Generally, detailed planning is associated with the science of control, including movement rates, fuel consumption, weapon effects, and time-distance factors. Detailed planning falls under the purview of the staff, focusing on specifics of execution. Detailed planning works out the scheduling, coordination, or technical problems involved with moving, sustaining, synchronizing, and directing the force.

2-19. The commander personally leads the conceptual component of planning. While commanders are engaged in parts of detailed planning, they often leave the specifics to the staff. Conceptual planning provides the basis for all subsequent planning. For example, the commander's intent and operational approach provide the framework for the entire plan. This framework leads to a concept of operations and associated schemes of support, such as schemes of intelligence, maneuver, fires, protection, and sustainment. In turn, the schemes of support lead to the specifics of execution, including tasks to subordinate units and detailed annexes to the operations plan or order. However, the dynamic does not operate in only one direction. Conceptual planning must respond to detailed constraints. For example, the realities of a deployment schedule (a detailed concern) influence the operational approach (a conceptual concern).

OPERATIONAL ART AND PLANNING

2-20. Conceptual planning is directly associated with *operational art*—the cognitive approach by commanders and staffs—supported by their skill, knowledge, experience, creativity, and judgment—to develop strategies, campaigns, and operations to organize and employ military forces by integrating ends, ways, and means (JP 3-0). Operational art is a thought process that guides conceptual and detailed planning to produce executable plans and orders.

Elements of operational art
• End state and conditions
• Center of gravity
• Decisive points
• Lines of operations and lines of effort
• Operational reach
• Basing
• Tempo
• Phasing and transitions
• Culmination
• Risk

2-21. In applying operational art, commanders and their staffs use a set of intellectual tools to help them communicate a common vision of the operational environment as well as visualizing and describing the operational approach. Collectively, this set of tools is known as the elements of operational art. These tools help commanders understand, visualize, and describe combinations of combat power and help them formulate their intent and guidance. Commanders selectively use these tools in any operation. However, their application is broadest in the context of long-term operations.

2-22. The elements of operational art support the commander in identifying objectives that link tactical missions to the desired end state. They help refine and focus the operational approach that forms the basis for developing a detailed plan or order. During execution, commanders and staffs consider the elements of operational art as they assess the situation. They adjust current and future operations and plans as the operation unfolds. (See ADRP 3-0 for a detailed discussion of each element of operational art.)

ARMY PLANNING METHODOLOGIES

2-23. Successful planning requires the integration of both conceptual and detailed thinking. Army leaders employ three methodologies for planning, determining the appropriate mix based on the scope of the problem, their familiarity with it, the time available, and the availability of a staff. Methodologies that assist commanders and staffs with planning include—

- Army design methodology.
- The military decisionmaking process (MDMP).
- Troop leading procedures (TLP).

ARMY DESIGN METHODOLOGY

2-24. *Army design methodology* is a methodology for applying critical and creative thinking to understand, visualize, and describe problems and approaches to solving them (ADP 5-0). Army design methodology is particularly useful as an aid to conceptual planning, but must be integrated with the detailed planning typically associated with the MDMP to produce executable plans. Key concepts that underline the Army design methodology include—

- Critical and creative thinking (see chapter 1).
- Collaboration and dialogue (see chapter 1).
- Framing.
- Narrative construction.
- Visual modeling.

Framing

2-25. Framing is the act of building mental models to help individuals understand situations and respond to events. Framing involves selecting, organizing, interpreting, and making sense of an operational environment and a problem by establishing context. How individuals or groups frame a problem will influence potential solutions. For example, an organization that frames an insurgent group as "freedom fighters" probably will approach solving a conflict differently from an organization that frames the insurgent group as "terrorists."

2-26. The Army design methodology involves deliberately framing an operational environment and problem through dialogue and critical and creative thinking by a group. The group considers the perspective and world views of others to understand the situation fully. This contextual understanding of an operational environment serves as a frame of reference for developing solutions to solve problems. Framing facilitates constructing hypotheses, or modeling, that focuses on the part of an operational environment or problem under consideration. Framing provides a perspective from which commanders and staffs can understand and act on a problem. Narrative construction and visual modeling facilitate framing.

Narrative Construction

2-27. In a broad sense, a narrative is a story constructed to give meaning to things and events. Individuals, groups, organizations, and countries all have narratives with many components that reflect and reveal how they define themselves. Political parties, social organizations, and government institutions, for example, all have stories bound chronologically and spatially. They incorporate symbols, historical events, and artifacts tied together with a logic that explains their reason for being. To narrate is to engage in the production of a story–an explanation of an event or phenomenon by proposing a question or questions in relation to the artifacts themselves. These questions may include—

- What is the meaning of what I see?
- Where does the story begin and end?
- What happened, is happening, and why?

2-28. Narrative construction—the conscious bounding of events and artifacts in time and space—is central to framing. Commanders, staffs, and unified action partners construct a narrative to help understand and explain the operational environment, the problem, and the solutions. Not only is the narrative useful in communicating to others, the act of constructing the narrative itself is a key learning event for the command.

Visual Modeling

2-29. Army design methodology relies heavily on forming and presenting ideas in both narrative and visual (graphic) form. Visual information tends to be stimulating; therefore, creativity can be enhanced by using visual models and constructs. The complexity of some problems requires creating a model of the problem. A visual model, based on logical inference from evidence, helps creative thought to develop into understanding. A graphic can often point to hidden relationships that were not considered through conversation alone. In addition, visually displaying periodic summaries of work helps individuals see the results of what is being thought. This, in turn, points to new ways of thinking and possible areas for further examination. In other words, seeing something drawn graphically helps individuals think through challenging problems, especially when examining abstract concepts.

ACTIVITIES OF THE ARMY DESIGN METHODOLOGY

2-30. Army design methodology entails framing an operational environment, framing a problem, and developing an operational approach to solve the problem. Army design methodology results in an improved understanding of the operational environment, a problem statement, initial commander's intent, and an operational approach that serves as the link between conceptual and detailed planning. Based on their understanding and learning gained during Army design methodology, commanders issue planning guidance, to include an operational approach, to guide more detailed planning using the MDMP.

2-31. The understanding developed through Army design methodology continues through preparation and execution in the form of continuous assessment. Assessment, to include updated running estimates, helps commanders measure the overall effectiveness of employing forces and capabilities to ensure that the operational approach remains feasible and acceptable within the context of the higher commander's intent and concept of operations. If the current operational approach fails to meet these criteria, or if aspects of the operational environment or problem change significantly, the commander may decide to reframe. Reframing involves revisiting earlier hypotheses, conclusions, and decisions that underpin the current operational approach. Reframing can lead to a new problem statement and operational approach, resulting in an entirely new plan.

2-32. Figure 2-2 depicts the general activities associated with Army design methodology. While planners complete some activities before others, the learning generated in one activity may require revisiting the learning derived in another activity. The movement between the activities is not entirely unidirectional, because what the commander, staff, and partners learn later will affect previous conclusions and decisions.

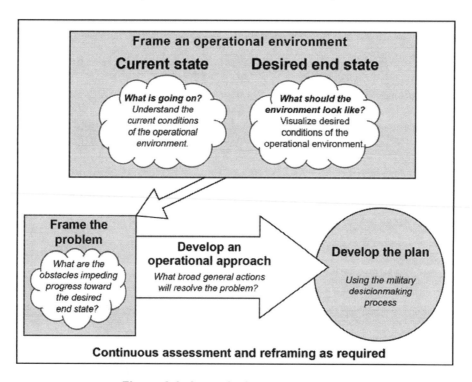

Figure 2-2. Army design methodology

Frame an Operational Environment

2-33. The commander, members of the staff, subordinate commanders, and unified action partners form a planning team to establish context for describing the problem and developing an operational approach by framing an operational environment. This framing facilitates hypothesizing, or modeling, that focuses on the part of the operational environment under consideration. Framing provides a perspective from which commanders can understand and act on a problem.

2-34. In framing an operational environment, the planning team focuses on defining, analyzing, and synthesizing the characteristics of the operational and mission variables (see chapter 1). Members of the planning team capture their work in an operational environmental frame (using narrative and visual models) that describes and depicts the history, culture, current state, relationships, and future goals of relevant actors in an operational environment. An operational environmental frame consists of two parts—the current state of the operational environment and the desired end state of the operational environment.

Current State of an Operational Environment

2-35. The commander and staff develop a contextual understanding of the situation by framing the current conditions of an operational environment. In doing so, the planning team considers the characteristics of all the operation and mission variables relevant to a particular operational environment. This includes identifying and explaining behaviors of relevant actors in the operational environment. An actor is an individual or group within a social network who acts to advance personal interests. Relevant actors may include individuals, states and governments, coalitions, terrorist networks, and criminal organizations. They may also include multinational corporations, nongovernmental organizations, and others able to influence the situation.

2-36. A diagram illustrating relevant actor relationships enables understanding and visualizing the operational environment. Often relationships among actors have many facets, and these relationships differ depending on the scale of interaction and temporal aspects (history, duration, type, and frequency). Clarifying the relationships among actors requires intense effort since these relationships must be examined from multiple perspectives. Commanders can also depict relationships by identifying and categorizing their unique characteristics. Figure 2-3 a sample presentation diagram of relevant actors and their relationships in the notional country of Newland.

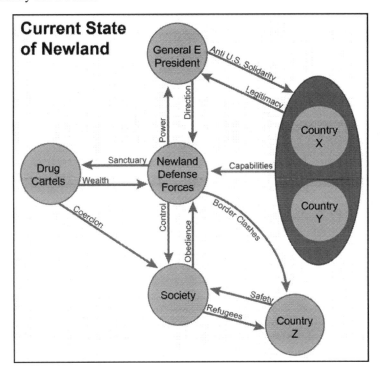

Figure 2-3. Sample presentation diagram of the current state of the operational environment

2-37. Figure 2-3 points out the links between key actors, what they exchange, and what they provide. [*Note*: Working diagrams would contain significantly more actors and relationships. The sample shown in figure 2-4 simplifies these working diagrams into what is known as a presentation diagram.] It depicts the current state of the operational environment under consideration. The sample narrative below provides further meaning to the graphic.

The Newland defense force controls the population and provides General E his power. The president, in turn, provides direction and power to the Newland defense force to control the society. The people are expected to comply with the direction provided by the president and the Newland defense forces. Those who do not comply are oppressed. In exchange for sanctuary, the drug cartels provide funding to the regime. They also harass and terrorize the section of the society that opposes the regime. Countries X and Y provide material capabilities to the Newland defense force and international legitimacy to the regime. In turn, the regime maintains an anti-U.S. policy stance. Over the last six months, over 100,000 persons have fled Newland to Country Z. Country Z is temporarily providing Newland refugees humanitarian assistance and protection. Several border clashes have erupted between Newland defense forces and Country Z in the last three weeks. The antidemocratic dictatorship of Newland that oppresses its people, encourages instability in the region, and supports criminal and terrorist activities is unacceptable to U.S. interests.

Desired End State of an Operational Environment

2-38. The second part of an operational environmental frame involves envisioning desired conditions of an operational environment (a desired end state). A desired end state consists of those desired conditions that, if achieved, meet the objectives of policy, orders, guidance, and directives issued by higher authorities. A condition is a reflection of the existing state of the operational environment. Thus, a desired condition is a sought-after future state of the operational environment.

2-39. Conditions may be tangible or intangible, military or nonmilitary. They may focus on physical or psychological factors. When describing conditions that constitute a desired end state, the commander considers their relevance to higher policy, orders, guidance, or directives. Since every operation focuses on a clearly defined, decisive, and attainable end state, success hinges on accurately describing those conditions. These conditions form the basis for decisions that ensure operations progress consistently toward a desired end state.

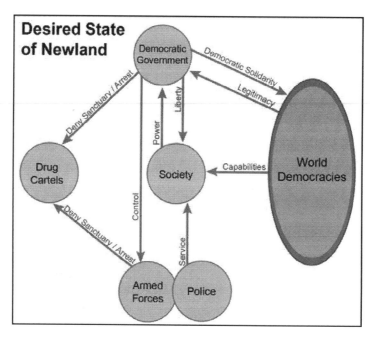

Figure 2-4. Sample presentation diagram of the desired current state of the operational environment

2-40. A method for envisioning a desired end state is to consider the natural tendencies and potential of relevant actors. Tendencies reflect the inclination to think or behave in a certain manner. Tendencies identify the likely pattern of relationships between the actors without external influence. Once identified, commanders and staffs evaluate the potential of these tendencies to manifest within the operational environment. Potential is the inherent ability or capacity for the growth or development of a specific interaction or relationship. Not all interactions and relationships support achieving a desired end state. A desired end state accounts for tendencies and potentials that exist among the relevant actors or other aspects of the operational variables in an operational environment frame. Figure 2-4 provides a sample presentation diagram of the desired end state of Newland. The following narrative supports the presentation diagram.

> The country of Newland is a friendly democracy that no longer oppresses its people, threatens its neighbors, or provides sanctuary for criminal and terrorist organizations. The society has replaced the Newland defense force as the source of power for the democratic government. The Newland defense force is replaced with an army and navy that serves the society and protects the country from external aggression. Local and national police forces serve the population by providing law and order for society. World democracies support the new government by providing legitimacy and capabilities to the government of Newland and the society. In turn, the new government of Newland supports the rule of law among nations and human rights.

Frame the Problem

2-41. A problem is an issue or obstacle that makes it difficult to achieve a desired goal or objective. In a broad sense, a problem exists when an individual becomes aware of a significant difference between what actually is and what is desired. In the context of operations, an operational problem is the issue or set of issues that impede commanders from achieving their desired end state. Problem framing involves identifying and understanding those issues that impede progress toward the desired end state.

2-42. The planning team frames the problem to ensure that they are solving the right problem, instead of solving the symptoms of the problem. Framing the problem involves understanding and isolating the root causes of conflict. The planning team closely examines the symptoms, the underlying tensions, and the root causes of conflict. Tension is the resistance or friction among and between actors. From this perspective, the planning team can identify the fundamental problem with greater clarity and consider more accurately how to solve it. A technique for framing the problem begins with two basic questions:

- What is the difference between the current state and the desired state of the operational environment?
- What is preventing US forces from reaching the desired end state?

Answers to these questions help identify the problem. For example, based on the operational environment frame of Newland, the planning team may start to ask—

- Is the problem General E?
- Is the problem the drug cartels?
- Is the problem the Newland defense force?

2-43. Based on the problem frame, the planning team develops a problem statement—a concise statement of the issue or issues requiring resolution. A potential problem statement based on the sample operational environment frame and problem frame of Newland follows:

> The Newland defense force is the primary impediment to establishing a democratic government in Newland and the primary factor of instability in the region. For over forty years, the Newland defense force has maintained power for itself and the regime by oppressing all opposition within society. In addition, the Newland defense force has a history of intimidating Country Z through force (both overtly and covertly). Corruption in the Newland defense force is rampant within the leadership, and it has close ties to several drug cartels. General E is the latest of two dictators emerging from the Newland defense force. Even if General E is removed from power, the potential of a new dictator emerging from the Newland defense force is likely. There is no indication that the leadership of the Newland defense force is willing to relinquish their power within Newland.

Develop an Operational Approach

2-44. Based on their understanding of the operational environment and the problem, the planning team considers operational approaches—the broad general actions—to solve the problem. The operational approach serves as the main idea that informs detailed planning and guides the force through preparation and execution.

2-45. The planning team uses the elements of operational art (see ADRP 3-0) to help think through the operational environment and visualize and describe the operational approach. As the planning team considers various approaches, it evaluates the types of defeat or stability mechanisms that may lead to conditions that define the desired end state. Thus, the operational approach enables commanders to begin visualizing and describing possible combinations of actions to reach the desired end state, given the tensions identified in the operational environment and problem frames. The staff uses operational approaches to develop courses of action during detailed planning.

2-46. Planners can depict the operational approach by using lines of effort that graphically articulate the links among tasks, objectives, conditions, and the desired end state (see figure 2-5). Army design methodology offers the latitude to portray the operational approach in a manner that best communicates its vision and structure. Ultimately, the commander determines the optimal method to articulate the operational approach. However, it is important that narratives accompany lines of effort to ensure subordinate commanders and Soldiers understand the operational approach.

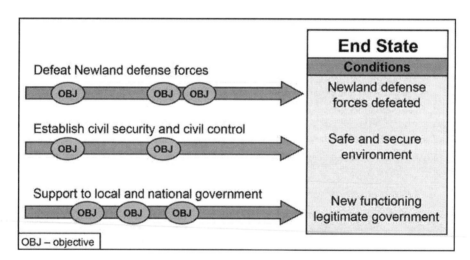

Figure 2-5. Sample operational approach depicted by lines of effort.

Document Results

2-47. Commanders and staffs document the results of Army design methodology to inform more detailed planning. Key outputs of Army design methodology conveyed in text and graphics include—

- Problem statement.
- Initial commander's intent.
- Planning guidance, to include an operational approach.

2-48. The problem statement generated during problem framing communicates the commander's understanding of the problem or problem set upon which the organization will act. The initial commander's intent describes the purpose of the operation, initial key tasks, and the desired end state. The operational approach organizes combinations of potential actions in time, space, and purpose that will guide the force to the desired end state. Planning guidance orients the focus of operations, linking desired conditions to potential combinations of actions the force may employ to achieve the desired end state.

Reframing

2-49. Through continuous assessment, the commander and staff monitor the operational environment and progress toward setting conditions and achieving objectives. Assessment helps commanders measure the overall effectiveness of employing forces and capabilities to ensure that the operational approach remains feasible and acceptable in the context of the higher commander's intent and concept of operations. If the current operational approach is failing to meet these criteria, or if aspects of the operational environment or problem change significantly, the commander may decide to begin reframing efforts.

2-50. Reframing is the activity of revisiting earlier design hypotheses, conclusions, and decisions that underpin the current operational approach. In essence, reframing reviews what the commander and staff believe they understand about the operational environment, the problem, and the desired end state. At any time during the operations process, the decision to reframe may be triggered by factors such as—

- Assessment reveals a lack of progress.
- Key assumptions prove invalid.
- Unanticipated success or failure.
- A major event that causes "catastrophic change" in the operational environment.
- A scheduled periodic review that shows a problem.
- A change in mission or end state issued by higher authority.

2-51. During operations, commanders decide to reframe after realizing the desired conditions have changed, are not achievable, cannot be attained through the current operational approach, or because of change of mission or end state. Reframing provides the freedom to operate beyond the limits of any single perspective. Conditions will change during execution, and such change is expected because forces interact within the operational environment. Recognizing and anticipating these changes is fundamental to Army design methodology and essential to an organization's ability to learn.

THE MILITARY DECISIONMAKING PROCESS

2-52. The *military decisionmaking process* is an iterative planning methodology to understand the situation and mission, develop a course of action, and produce an operation plan or order (ADP 5-0). The military decisionmaking process (MDMP) integrates the activities of the commander, staff, subordinate headquarters, and unified action partners to understand the situation and mission; develop and compare courses of action; decide on a course of action that best accomplishes the mission; and produce an operation plan or order for execution. The MDMP helps leaders apply thoroughness, clarity, sound judgment, logic, and professional knowledge to understand situations, develop options to solve problems, and reach decisions. This process helps commanders, staffs, and others think critically and creatively while planning. The MDMP results in an improved understanding of the situation and a plan or order that guides the force through preparation and execution.

2-53. The MDMP consists of seven steps as shown in figure 2-6 on page 2-12. Each step of the MDMP has various inputs, a method (step) to conduct, and outputs. The outputs lead to an increased understanding of the situation and to facilitating the next step of the MDMP. Commanders and staffs generally perform these steps sequentially; however, they may revisit several steps in an iterative fashion, as they learn more about the situation before producing the plan or order.

2-54. Commanders initiate the MDMP upon receipt of or in anticipation of a mission. Commanders and staffs often begin planning in the absence of a complete and approved higher headquarters' operation plan (OPLAN) or operation order (OPORD). In these instances, the headquarters begins a new planning effort based on a warning order (WARNO) and other directives, such as a planning order or an alert order from their higher headquarters. This requires active collaboration with the higher headquarters and parallel planning among echelons as the plan or order is developed.

2-55. The MDMP facilitates collaboration and parallel planning. The higher headquarters solicits input and continuously shares information concerning future operations through planning meetings, warning orders, and other means. It shares information with subordinate and adjacent units, supporting and supported units, and other military and civilian partners. Commanders encourage active collaboration among all organizations affected by the pending operations to build a shared understanding of the situation, participate in course of action development and decisionmaking, and resolve conflicts before publishing the plan or order.

Key inputs	Steps	Key outputs
• Higher headquarters' plan or order or a new mission anticipated by the commander	Step 1: Receipt of Mission	• Commander's initial guidance • Initial allocation of time
	Warning order	
• Higher headquarters' plan or order • Higher headquarters' knowledge and intelligence products • Knowledge products from other organizations • Army design methodology products	Step 2: Mission Analysis	• Problem statement • Mission statement • Initial commander's intent • Initial planning guidance • Initial CCIRs and EEFIs • Updated IPB and running estimates • Assumptions
	Warning order	
• Mission statement • Initial commander's intent, planning guidance, CCIRs, and EEFIs • Updated IPB and running estimates • Assumptions	Step 3: Course of Action (COA) Development	• COA statements and sketches - Tentative task organization - Broad concept of operations • Revised planning guidance • Updated assumptions
• Updated running estimates • Revised planning guidance • COA statements and sketches • Updated assumptions	Step 4: COA Analysis (War Game)	• Refined COAs • Potential decision points • War-game results • Initial assessment measures • Updated assumptions
• Updated running estimates • Refined COAs • Evaluation criteria • War-game results • Updated assumptions	Step 5: COA Comparison	• Evaluated COAs • Recommended COAs • Updated running estimates • Updated assumptions
• Updated running estimates • Evaluated COAs • Recommended COA • Updated assumptions	Step 6: COA Approval	• Commander-selected COA and any modifications • Refined commander's intent, CCIRs, and EEFIs • Updated assumptions
	Warning order	
• Commander-selected COA with any modifications • Refined commander's intent, CCIRs, and EEFIs • Updated assumptions	Step 7: Orders Production, Dissemination, and Transition	• Approved operation plan or order • Subordinates understand the plan or order

CCIR commander's critical information requirement EEFI essential element of friendly information
COA course of action IPB intelligence preparation of the battlefield

Figure 2-6. Steps of the military decisionmaking process

2-56. The MDMP also drives preparation. Since time is a factor in all operations, commanders and staffs conduct a time analysis early in the planning process. This analysis helps them determine what actions they need and when to begin those actions to ensure forces are ready and in position before execution. This may require the commander to direct subordinates to start necessary movements, conduct task organization changes, begin surveillance and reconnaissance operations, and execute other preparation activities before completing the plan. As the commander and staff conduct the MDMP, they direct the tasks in a series of WARNOs.

2-57. The commander is the most important participant in the MDMP. More than simply decisionmakers in this process, commanders use their experience, knowledge, and judgment to guide staff planning efforts. While unable to devote all their time to the MDMP, commanders follow the status of the planning effort, participate during critical periods of the process, and make decisions based on the detailed work of the staff. During the MDMP, commanders focus their activities on understanding, visualizing, and describing.

2-58. The MDMP stipulates several formal meetings and briefings between the commander and staff to discuss, assess, and approve or disapprove planning efforts as they progress. However, experience has shown that optimal planning results when the commander meets informally at frequent intervals with the staff throughout the MDMP. Such informal interaction between the commander and staff can improve the staff's understanding of the situation and ensure the staff's planning effort adequately reflects the commander's visualization of the operation.

2-59. The chief of staff (COS) or executive officer (XO) is a key participant in the MDMP. The COS or XO manages and coordinates the staff's work and provides quality control during the MDMP. To effectively supervise the entire process, this officer clearly understands the commander's intent and guidance. The COS or XO provides timelines to the staff, establishes briefing times and locations, and provides any instructions necessary to complete the plan.

2-60. The staff's effort during the MDMP focuses on helping the commander understand the situation, make decisions, and synchronize those decisions into a fully developed plan or order. Staff activities during planning initially focus on mission analysis. The products that the staff develops during mission analysis help commanders understand the situation and develop the commander's visualization. During course of action (COA) development and COA comparison, the staff provides recommendations to support the commander in selecting a COA. After the commander makes a decision, the staff prepares the plan or order that reflects the commander's intent, coordinating all necessary details.

ARMY DESIGN METHODOLOGY AND THE MILITARY DECISIONMAKING PROCESS

2-61. Depending on the situation—to include the familiarity of the problem—commanders conduct Army design methodology before, in parallel with, or after the MDMP. When faced with an unfamiliar problem or when developing initial plans for extended operations, commanders often initiate the Army design methodology before the MDMP. This sequence helps them better understand the operational environment, frame the problem, and develop an operational approach to guide more detailed planning.

2-62. Commanders may also elect to conduct the Army design methodology in parallel with the MDMP. In this instance, members of the staff conduct mission analysis as the commander and other staff members engage in framing the operational environment and the problem. This focus helps commanders better understand aspects of the operational environment. The results of mission analysis (to include intelligence preparation of the battlefield and running estimates) inform commanders as they develop their operational approach that, in turn, facilitates course of action development during the MDMP.

2-63. In time-constrained conditions requiring immediate action, or if the problem is familiar, commanders may conduct the MDMP and publish an operation order without formally conducting Army design methodology. As time becomes available during execution, commanders may then initiate Army design methodology to help refine their commander's visualization and the initial plan developed using the MDMP.

TROOP LEADING PROCEDURES

2-64. Troop leading procedures extend the MDMP to the small-unit level. The MDMP and troop leading procedures (TLP) are similar but not identical. Commanders with a coordinating staff use the MDMP as their primary planning process. Company-level and smaller units lack formal staffs and use TLP to plan and prepare for operations. This places the responsibility for planning primarily on the commander or small-unit leader.

2-65. *Troop leading procedures* are a dynamic process used by small-unit leaders to analyze a mission, develop a plan, and prepare for an operation (ADP 5-0). These procedures enable leaders to maximize available planning time while developing effective plans and preparing their units for an operation. TLP consist of eight steps. The sequence of the steps of TLP is not rigid. Leaders modify the sequence to meet the mission, situation, and available time. Leaders perform some steps concurrently, while other steps may be performed continuously throughout the operation. The eight steps are:

- Step 1 – Receive the mission.
- Step 2 – Issue a warning order.
- Step 3 – Make a tentative plan.
- Step 4 – Initiate movement.
- Step 5 – Conduct reconnaissance.
- Step 6 – Complete the plan.
- Step 7 – Issue the order.
- Step 8 – Supervise and refine.

2-66. Leaders use TLP when working alone or with a small group to solve tactical problems. For example, a company commander may use the executive officer, first sergeant, fire support officer, supply sergeant, and communications sergeant to assist during TLP.

2-67. Leaders begin TLP when they receive the initial WARNO or receive a new mission. As each subsequent order arrives, leaders modify their assessments, update tentative plans, and continue to supervise and assess preparations. In some situations, the higher headquarters may not issue the full sequence of WARNOs; security considerations or tempo may make it impractical. Commanders carefully consider decisions to eliminate WARNOs. Subordinate units always need to have enough information to plan and prepare for an operation. In other cases, leaders may initiate TLP before receiving a WARNO based on existing plans and orders (contingency plans or be-prepared missions) and on their understanding of the situation.

2-68. Parallel planning hinges on distributing information as it is received or developed. Leaders cannot complete their plans until they receive their unit mission. If each successive WARNO contains enough information, the higher headquarters' final order will confirm what subordinate leaders have already analyzed and put into their tentative plans. In other cases, the higher headquarters' order may change or modify the subordinate's tasks enough that additional planning and reconnaissance are required.

KEY COMPONENTS OF A PLAN

2-69. The unit's task organization, mission statement, commander's intent, concept of operations, tasks to subordinate units, coordinating instructions, and control measures are key components of a plan. Commanders ensure their mission and end state nest with those of their higher headquarters. While the commander's intent focuses on the end state, the concept of operations focuses on the way or sequence of actions by which the force will achieve the end state. The concept of operations expands on the mission statement and commander's intent. Within the concept of operations, commanders may establish objectives as intermediate goals toward achieving the operation's end state. When developing tasks for subordinate units, commanders ensure that the purpose of each task nests with the accomplishment of another task, with the achievement of an objective, or directly to the attainment of an end state condition.

TASK ORGANIZATION

2-70. *Task organization* **is a temporary grouping of forces designed to accomplish a particular mission.** Commanders task organize the force by establishing command and support relationships. Command relationships define command responsibility and authority. Support relationships define the purpose, scope, and effect desired when one capability supports another. The unit's task organization is in the base plan or order or in Annex A (Task Organization).

Note: Army support relationships are similar but not identical to joint support relationships. (See JP 3-0 for a discussion of joint command and support relationships.)

2-71. Establishing clear command and support relationships is fundamental to organizing for any operation. These relationships establish clear responsibilities and authorities between subordinate and supporting units. Some command relationships (for example, tactical control) limit the commander's authority to prescribe additional relationships. Knowing the inherent responsibilities of each command and support relationship allows commanders to organize their forces effectively and helps supporting commanders to understand their unit's role in the organizational structure.

2-72. Commanders designate command and support relationships to weight the decisive operation and support the concept of operations. These relationships carry with them varying responsibilities to the subordinate unit by the parent and gaining units as listed in table 2-1 on page 2-16 and table 2-2 on page 2-18. Commanders consider two organizational principles when task-organizing forces:

- Maintain cohesive mission teams.
- Do not exceed subordinates' span of control capabilities.

2-73. When possible, commanders maintain cohesive mission teams. They organize forces based on standing headquarters, their assigned forces, and habitual associations when possible. When this is not feasible and commanders create ad hoc organizations, they arrange time for training and establishing functional working relationships and procedures. Once commanders have organized and committed a force, they keep its task organization unless the advantages of a change clearly outweigh the disadvantages. Reorganizations may result in a loss of time, effort, and tempo. Sustainment considerations may also preclude quick reorganization.

2-74. Commanders carefully avoid exceeding the span of control capabilities of subordinates. Span of control refers to the number of subordinate units under a single commander. This number is situation dependent and may vary. As a rule, commanders can effectively command two to six subordinate units. Allocating subordinate commanders more units gives them greater flexibility and increases options and combinations. However, increasing the number of subordinate units increases the number of decisions the commander must make and may decrease agility.

Army Command Relationships

2-75. Table 2-1 on page 2-16 lists the Army command relationships. Command relationships define superior and subordinate relationships between unit commanders. By specifying a chain of command, command relationships unify effort and enable commanders to use subordinate forces with maximum flexibility. Army command relationships identify the degree of control of the gaining Army commander. The type of command relationship often relates to the expected longevity of the relationship between the headquarters involved and quickly identifies the degree of support that the gaining and losing Army commanders provide. Army command relationships include organic, assigned, attached, operational control (OPCON), tactical control (TACON), and administrative control (ADCON).

2-76. *Organic* forces are those assigned to and forming an essential part of a military organization. Organic parts of a unit are those listed in its table of organization for the Army, Air Force, and Marine Corps, and are assigned to the administrative organizations of the operating forces for the Navy (JP 1-02). Joint command relationships do not include organic because a joint force commander is not responsible for the organizational structure of units. That is a Service responsibility.

Table 2-1. Army command relationships

If relation-ship is:	Then inherent responsibilities:							
	Have command relation-ship with:	May be task-organized by:[1]	Unless modified, ADCON responsi-bility goes through:	Are assigned position or AO by:	Provide liaison to:	Establish/ maintain communi-cations with:	Have priorities establish-ed by:	Can impose on gaining unit further command or support relationship of:
Organic	All organic forces organized with the HQ	Organic HQ	Army HQ specified in organizing document	Organic HQ	N/A	N/A	Organic HQ	Attached; OPCON; TACON; GS; GSR; R; DS
Assigned	Combatant command	Gaining HQ	Gaining Army HQ	OPCON chain of command	As required by OPCON	As required by OPCON	ASCC or Service-assigned HQ	As required by OPCON HQ
Attached	Gaining unit	Gaining unit	Gaining Army HQ	Gaining unit	As required by gaining unit	Unit to which attached	Gaining unit	Attached; OPCON; TACON; GS; GSR; R; DS
OPCON	Gaining unit	Parent unit and gaining unit; gaining unit may pass OPCON to lower HQ[1]	Parent unit	Gaining unit	As required by gaining unit	As required by gaining unit and parent unit	Gaining unit	OPCON; TACON; GS; GSR; R; DS
TACON	Gaining unit	Parent unit	Parent unit	Gaining unit	As required by gaining unit	As required by gaining unit and parent unit	Gaining unit	TACON;GS GSR; R; DS

Note: [1] In NATO, the gaining unit may not task-organize a multinational force. (See TACON.)

ADCON	administrative control	HQ	headquarters
AO	area of operations	N/A	not applicable
ASCC	Army Service component command	NATO	North Atlantic Treaty Organization
DS	direct support	OPCON	operational control
GS	general support	R	reinforcing
GSR	general support–reinforcing	TACON	tactical control

2-77. The Army establishes organic command relationships through organizational documents such as tables of organization and equipment and tables of distribution and allowances. If temporarily task-organized with another headquarters, organic units return to the control of their organic headquarters after completing the mission. To illustrate, within a brigade combat team, the entire brigade is organic. In contrast, within most modular support brigades, there is a "base" of organic battalions and companies and a variable mix of assigned and attached battalions and companies.

2-78. *Assign* is to place units or personnel in an organization where such placement is relatively permanent, and/or where such organization controls and administers the units or personnel for the primary function, or greater portion of the functions, of the unit or personnel (JP 3-0). Unless specifically stated, this relationship includes ADCON.

2-79. *Attach* is the placement of units or personnel in an organization where such placement is relatively temporary (JP 3-0). A unit that is temporarily placed into an organization is attached.

2-80. *Operational control* is a command authority that may be exercised by commanders at any echelon at or below the level of combatant command. Operational control is inherent in combatant command (command authority) and may be delegated within the command. Operational control is the authority to perform those functions of command over subordinate forces involving organizing and employing commands and forces, assigning tasks, designating objectives, and giving authoritative direction necessary to accomplish the mission. Operational control includes authoritative direction over all aspects of military operations and joint training necessary to accomplish missions assigned to the command. Operational control should be exercised through the commanders of subordinate organizations. Normally this authority is exercised through subordinate joint force commanders and Service and/or functional component commanders. Operational control normally provides full authority to organize commands and forces and to employ those forces as the commander in operational control considers necessary to accomplish assigned missions; it does not, in and of itself, include authoritative direction for logistics or matters of administration, discipline, internal organization, or unit training (JP 3-0).

2-81. *Tactical control* is a command authority over assigned or attached forces or commands, or military capability or forces made available for tasking, that is limited to the detailed direction and control of movements or maneuvers within the operational area necessary to accomplish missions or tasks assigned. Tactical control is inherent in operational control. Tactical control may be delegated to, and exercised at any level at or below the level of combatant command. Tactical control provides sufficient authority for controlling and directing the application of force or tactical use of combat support assets within the assigned mission or task (JP 3-0). Tactical control allows commanders below combatant command level to apply force and direct the tactical use of logistic assets, but it does not provide authority to change organizational structure or direct administrative and logistical support.

2-82. When commanders establish command relationships, they determine if the command relationship includes ADCON. *Administrative control* is the direction or exercise of authority over subordinate or other organizations in respect to administration and support, including organization of Service forces, control of resources and equipment, personnel management, unit logistics, individual and unit training, readiness, mobilization, demobilization, discipline, and other matters not included in the operational missions of the subordinate or other organizations (JP 1).

2-83. ADCON is equivalent to administration and support responsibilities identified in Title 10 United States Code. This is the authority necessary to fulfill military department statutory responsibilities for administration and support. ADCON of an Army unit must remain in Army channels. It cannot be transferred to a unit of another Service.

2-84. Attachment orders normally state whether the parent unit retains ADCON of the unit. If it does not, the attachment order specifically states that the gaining unit has ADCON. For OPCON and TACON, parent units retain ADCON.

Army Support Relationships

2-85. Table 2-2 on page 2-18 lists Army support relationships. Army support relationships are direct support (DS), general support (GS), reinforcing (R), and general support-reinforcing (GSR). Army support relationships are not command authorities and are more specific than joint support relationships. Commanders establish support relationships when subordination of one unit to another is inappropriate. Commanders assign a support relationship when—

- The support is more effective if a commander with the requisite technical and tactical expertise controls the supporting unit rather than the supported commander.
- The echelon of the supporting unit is the same as or higher than that of the supported unit. For example, the supporting unit may be a brigade, and the supported unit may be a battalion. It would be inappropriate for the brigade to be subordinated to the battalion; hence, the echelon uses an Army support relationship.
- The supporting unit supports several units simultaneously. The requirement to set support priorities to allocate resources to supported units exists. Assigning support relationships is one aspect of mission command.

2-86. Army support relationships allow supporting commanders to employ their units' capabilities to achieve results required by supported commanders. Support relationships are graduated from an exclusive supported and supporting relationship between two units—as in direct support—to a broad level of support extended to all units under the control of the higher headquarters—as in general support. Support relationships do not alter administrative control. Commanders specify and change support relationships through task organization

Table 2-2. Army support relationships

If relation-ship is:	Then inherent responsibilities:							
	Have command relation-ship with:	May be task-organized by:	Receives sustain-ment from:	Are assigned position or an area of operations by:	Provide liaison to:	Establish/ maintain communi-cations with:	Have priorities established by:	Can impose on gaining unit further command or support relation-ship by:
Direct support¹	Parent unit	Parent unit	Parent unit	Supported unit	Supported unit	Parent unit; supported unit	Supported unit	See note¹
Reinforc-ing	Parent unit	Parent unit	Parent unit	Reinforced unit	Reinforced unit	Parent unit; reinforced unit	Reinforced unit; then parent unit	Not applicable
General support– reinforc-ing	Parent unit	Parent unit	Parent unit	Parent unit	Reinforced unit and as required by parent unit	Reinforced unit and as required by parent unit	Parent unit; then reinforced unit	Not applicable
General support	Parent unit	Parent unit	Parent unit	Parent unit	As required by parent unit	As required by parent unit	Parent unit	Not applicable

Note: ¹Commanders of units in direct support may further assign support relationships between their subordinate units and elements of the supported unit after coordination with the supported commander.

2-87. *Direct support* **is a support relationship requiring a force to support another specific force and authorizing it to answer directly to the supported force's request for assistance.** (Joint doctrine considers direct support (DS) as a mission rather than a support relationship). A unit assigned a DS relationship retains its command relationship with its parent unit, but is positioned by and has priorities of support established by the supported unit.

2-88. *General support* is that support which is given to the supported force as a whole and not to any particular subdivision thereof (JP 3-09.3). Units assigned a GS relationship are positioned and have priorities established by their parent unit.

2-89. *Reinforcing* **is a support relationship requiring a force to support another supporting unit.** Only like units (for example, artillery to artillery) can be given a reinforcing mission. A unit assigned a reinforcing support relationship retains its command relationship with its parent unit, but is positioned by the reinforced unit. A unit that is reinforcing has priorities of support established by the reinforced unit, then the parent unit.

2-90. *General support-reinforcing* **is a support relationship assigned to a unit to support the force as a whole and to reinforce another similar-type unit**. A unit assigned a general support-reinforcing (GSR) support relationship is positioned and has priorities established by its parent unit and secondly by the reinforced unit.

MISSION STATEMENT

2-91. The *mission* is the task, together with the purpose, that clearly indicates the action to be taken and the reason therefore (JP 3-0). Commanders analyze a mission as the commander's intent two echelons above them, specified tasks, and implied tasks. They also consider the mission of adjacent units to understand how they contribute to the decisive operation of their higher headquarters. Results of that analysis yield the essential tasks that—with the purpose of the operation—clearly specify the action required. This analysis produces the unit's mission statement—a clear statement of the action to be taken and the reason for taking it. The mission statement contains the elements of who, what, when, where, and why, but seldom specifies how. The format for writing a task to subordinate units also follows this format.

COMMANDER'S INTENT

2-92. The commander's intent succinctly describes what constitutes success for the operation. It includes the operation's purpose, key tasks, and the conditions that define the end state. It links the mission, concept of operations, and tasks to subordinate units. A clear commander's intent facilitates a shared understanding and focuses on the overall conditions that represent mission accomplishment. During execution, the commander's intent spurs disciplined initiative.

2-93. The commander's intent must be easy to remember and clearly understood by leaders and Soldiers two echelons lower in the chain of command. The shorter the commander's intent, the better it serves these purposes. Commanders develop their intent statement personally using the following components:

- Expanded purpose.
- Key tasks.
- End state.

2-94. When describing the expanded purpose of the operations, the commander's intent does not restate the "why" of the mission statement. Rather, it addresses the broader purpose of the operations and its relationship to the force as a whole.

2-95. *Key tasks* **are those activities the force must perform as a whole to achieve the desired end state**. Key tasks are not specified tasks for any subordinate unit; however, they may be sources of implied tasks. Acceptable courses of action accomplish all key tasks. During execution—when significant opportunities present themselves or the concept of operations no longer fits the situation—subordinates use key tasks to keep their efforts focused on achieving the desired end state. Examples of key tasks include terrain the force must control or an effect the force must have on the enemy.

2-96. The end state is a set of desired future conditions the commander wants to exist when an operation is concluded. Commanders describe the operation's end state by stating the desired conditions of the friendly force in relationship to desired conditions of the enemy, terrain, and civil considerations. A clearly defined end state promotes unity of effort among the force and with unified action partners.

CONCEPT OF OPERATIONS

2-97. The *concept of operations* **is a statement that directs the manner in which subordinate units cooperate to accomplish the mission and establishes the sequence of actions the force will use to achieve the end state**. The concept of operations expands on the commander's intent by describing how the commander wants the force to accomplish the mission. It states the principal tasks required, the responsible subordinate units, and how the principal tasks complement one another. Commanders and staff use the following operational frameworks to help conceptualize and describe their concept of operation:

- Deep-close-security.
- Decisive-shaping-sustaining.
- Main and supporting effort.

ADRP 3-0 discusses each framework in detail.

2-98. In addition to the operational frameworks, commanders and staffs consider nested concepts, the sequence of actions and phasing, decisive points and objectives, and lines of operations and lines of effort when conceptualizing and describing the concept of operations.

Nested Concepts

2-99. *Nested concepts* is a planning technique to achieve unity of purpose whereby each succeeding echelon's concept of operations is aligned by purpose with the higher echelons' concept of operations. An effective concept of operations describes how the forces will support the mission of the higher headquarters and how the actions of subordinate units fit together to accomplish the mission. Commanders do this by organizing their forces by purpose. Commanders ensure that the primary tasks for each subordinate unit include a purpose that links the completion of that task to achievement of another task, an objective, or an end state condition.

Sequencing Actions and Phasing

2-100. Part of the art of planning is determining the sequence of actions that best accomplishes the mission. The concept of operations describes in sequence the start of the operation to the projected status of the force at the operation's end. If the situation dictates a significant change in tasks, task organization, or priorities of support during the operation, the commander may phase the operation. A *phase* is a planning and execution tool used to divide an operation in duration or activity (ADRP 3-0). For each phase of an operation, the commander designates a main effort. (See JP 5-0 for a discussion of phasing joint operations.)

2-101. Ideally, commanders plan to accomplish the mission with simultaneous actions throughout the area of operations. However, resource constraints and the friendly force's size may hinder the commanders' ability to do this. In these cases, commanders phase the operation. A change in phase usually involves a combination of changes of mission, task organization, priorities of support, or rules of engagement. Phasing helps in planning and controlling, and phasing may be indicated by time, distance, terrain, or event.

Decisive Points and Objectives

2-102. Identifying decisive points and determining objectives are central to creating the concept of operations. A *decisive point* is a geographic place, specific key event, critical factor, or function that, when acted upon, allows commanders to gain a marked advantage over an adversary or contribute materially to achieving success (JP 3-0). Examples of potential geographic decisive points include port facilities, towns controlling key road networks, distribution networks and nodes, and bases of operations. Specific events and elements of an enemy force may also be decisive points, such as commitment of a reserve or unit that delivers weapons of mass destruction. Decisive points have a different character during operations dominated by stability. These decisive points may be less tangible and more closely associated with important events and conditions. Examples include, but are not limited to—

- Participation in elections by a certain group.
- Electric power restored in a certain area.
- Police and emergency services reestablished.

2-103. Often, a situation presents more decisive points than the force can act on. The art of planning includes selecting decisive points that best lead to mission accomplishment and acting on them in a sequence that most quickly and efficiently leads to mission success. Once identified for action, decisive points become objectives.

2-104. An objective can be physical (an enemy force or terrain feature) or conceptual in the form of a goal (rule of law established). In the physical sense, an *objective* is a location on the ground used to orient operations, phase operations, facilitate changes of direction, and provide for unity of effort (FM 3-90). In the conceptual sense, an *objective* is the clearly defined, decisive, and attainable goal toward which every operation is directed (JP 5-0). Objectives provide the basis for determining tasks to subordinate units. The most important objective forms the basis for developing the decisive operation.

Lines of Operations and Lines of Effort

2-105. Lines of operations and lines of effort are two key elements of operational art that assist in developing a concept of operations. Combat operations are typically designed using lines of operations. These lines tie tasks to the geographic and positional references in the area of operations. Commanders synchronize activities along complementary lines of operations to achieve the desired end state. (See ADRP 3-0.)

2-106. The line of effort is a useful tool for developing the concept of operations when stability operations or defense support to civil authorities dominate. Lines of effort link multiple tasks with goal-oriented objectives that focus efforts toward establishing end state conditions. Using lines of effort is essential in planning when positional references to an enemy or adversary have little relevance.

2-107. Lines of operations and lines of effort link objectives to the end state. Commanders may describe an operation along lines of operations, lines of effort, or a combination of both. The combination of them may change based on the conditions within the area of operations. Commanders synchronize and sequence actions, deliberately creating complementary and reinforcing effects. The lines then converge on the well-defined, commonly understood end state outlined in the commander's intent.

2-108. Commanders at all levels may use lines of operations and lines of effort to develop tasks and to allocate resources. Commanders may designate one line as the decisive operation and others as shaping operations. Commanders synchronize and sequence related actions along multiple lines. Seeing these relationships helps commanders assess progress toward achieving the end state as forces perform tasks and accomplish missions.

Lines of Operations

2-109. A *line of operations* is a line that defines the directional orientation of a force in time and space in relation to the enemy and links the force with its base of operations and objectives (ADRP 3-0). Lines of operations connect a series of tasks that lead to control of a geographic or force-oriented objective. Operations designed using lines of operations generally consist of a series of actions executed according to a well-defined sequence. These lines tie offensive and defensive tasks to the geographic and positional references in the area of operations.

Lines of Effort

2-110. A *line of effort* is a line that links multiple tasks using the logic of purpose rather than geographical reference to focus efforts toward establishing operational and strategic conditions (ADRP 3-0). The line of effort is a useful tool for developing the concept of operations when stability or defense support to civil authorities operations dominate. Lines of effort link multiple tasks with goal-oriented objectives that focus efforts toward establishing end state conditions. Using lines of effort is essential in planning when positional references to an enemy or adversary have little relevance. (See figure 2-5 on page 2-10 for an example of an operational approach depicted by lines of effort.)

Tasks to Subordinate Units

2-111. Tasks to subordinate units direct individual units to perform a specific action. Tasks are specific activities that contribute to accomplishing missions or other requirements. Tasks direct friendly action. The purpose of each task should nest with completing another task, achieving an objective, or attaining an end state condition.

2-112. When developing tasks for subordinate units, commanders and staffs use the same who, what (task), when, where, and why (purpose) construct that they did to develop the unit's mission statement. Sometimes commanders may want to specify the type or form of operation to use to accomplish a task. For example, the commander may direct an infiltration to avoid tipping off the enemy and to synchronize the timing of the unit's tasks with other units' tasks.

Coordinating Instructions

2-113. Coordinating instructions apply to two or more units. They are located in the coordinating instructions subparagraph of paragraph 3 (execution) of plans or orders. Examples include CCIRs, fire support coordination and airspace coordinating measures, rules of engagement, risk mitigation measures, and the time or condition when the operation order becomes effective.

Control Measures

2-114. Commanders exercise control through control measures established throughout an OPLAN or OPORD. A *control measure* is a means of regulating forces or warfighting functions (ADP 6-0). Control measures are established under a commander's authority; however, commanders may authorize staff officers and subordinate leaders to establish them. Commanders may use control measures for several purposes: for example, to assign responsibilities, require synchronization between forces, impose restrictions, or establish guidelines to regulate freedom of action. Control measures are essential to coordinating subordinates' actions. They can be permissive or restrictive. Permissive control measures allow specific actions to occur; restrictive control measures limit the conduct of certain actions.

2-115. Control measures help commanders direct actions by establishing responsibilities and limits that prevent subordinate units' actions from impeding one another. They foster coordination and cooperation between forces without unnecessarily restricting freedom of action. Good control measures foster freedom of action, decisionmaking, and individual initiative.

2-116. Control measures may be detailed (such as a division operation order) or simple (such as a checkpoint). Control measures include, but are not limited to—
- Laws and regulations.
- Planning guidance.
- Delegation of authority.
- Specific instructions to plans and orders and their elements, including—
  - Commander's intent.
  - Unit missions and tasks.
  - CCIRs.
  - EEFIs.
  - Task organization.
  - Concept of operations.
  - Target lists.
  - Rules of engagement.
  - Graphic control measures.
  - Unit standard operating procedures that control actions such as reporting and battle rhythm.

2-117. Certain control measures belong to the commander alone and may not be delegated. These include the commander's intent, unit mission statement, planning guidance, CCIRs, and EEFIs. Unit standard operating procedures specify many control measures. An operation plan or order modifies them and adds additional measures for a specific operation. Commanders, assisted by their staffs, modify control measures to account for the dynamic conditions of operations.

2-118. Some control measures are graphic. A *graphic control measure* is a symbol used on maps and displays to regulate forces and warfighting functions (ADRP 6-0). Graphic control measures are always prescriptive. They include symbols for boundaries, fire support coordination measures, some airspace control measures, air defense areas, and minefields. Commanders establish them to regulate maneuver, movement, airspace use, fires, and other aspects of operations. In general, all graphic control measures should relate to easily identifiable natural or man-made terrain features. (FM 1-02 portrays and defines graphic control measures and discusses rules for selecting and applying them.)

GUIDES TO EFFECTIVE PLANNING

2-119. Planning helps commanders understand and develop solutions to problems, anticipate events, adapt to changing circumstances, task-organize the force, and prioritize efforts. Effective planning requires dedication, study, and practice. Planners must be technically and tactically competent within their areas of expertise and disciplined in the use of doctrinally correct terms and symbols. The following guides aid in effective planning:
- Commanders focus planning.
- Develop simple, flexible plans through mission orders.

- Optimize available planning time.
- Continually refine the plan.

COMMANDERS FOCUS PLANNING

2-120. Commanders are the most important participants in effective planning. They focus the planning effort by providing their commander's intent, issuing planning guidance, and making decisions throughout the planning process. Commanders apply discipline to the planning process to meet the requirements of time, planning horizons, simplicity, level of detail, and desired outcomes. Commanders ensure that all operation plans and orders comply with domestic and international laws. They also confirm that the plan or order is relevant and suitable for subordinates. Generally, the more involved commanders are in planning, the faster staffs can plan. Through personal involvement, commanders ensure the plan reflects their commander's intent.

DEVELOP SIMPLE, FLEXIBLE PLANS THROUGH MISSION ORDERS

2-121. Effective plans and orders are simple and direct. Staffs prepare clear, concise orders that communicate a clear understanding of the operation through the use of doctrinally correct operational terms and symbols. Doing this minimizes chances of misunderstanding. Clarity and brevity are key components of effective plans. Developing shorter, rather than longer, plans aids in maintaining simplicity. Shorter plans are easier to disseminate, read, and remember.

2-122. Flexible plans help units adapt quickly to changing circumstances. Commanders and planners build opportunities for initiative into plans by anticipating events. This allows them to operate inside of the enemy's decision cycle or to react promptly to deteriorating situations. Identifying decision points and designing branches ahead of time—combined with a clear commander's intent—help create flexible plans.

2-123. Commanders stress the importance of using mission orders as a way of building simple, flexible plans. *Mission orders* are directives that emphasize to subordinates the results to be attained, not how they are to achieve them (ADP 6-0). Mission orders clearly convey the unit's mission and the commander's intent. Mission orders focus subordinates on what to do and the purpose of doing it, without prescribing exactly how to do it. Commanders establish control measures to aid cooperation among forces without imposing needless restriction on freedom of action.

OPTIMIZE AVAILABLE PLANNING TIME

2-124. Time is a critical variable in operations. Therefore, time management is important in planning. Whether done deliberately or rapidly, all planning requires the skillful use of available time to optimize planning and preparation throughout the unit. Taking more time to plan often results in greater synchronization; however, any delay in execution risks yielding the initiative—with more time to prepare and act—to the enemy. When allocating planning time to staffs, commanders must ensure subordinates have enough time to plan and prepare their own actions prior to execution. Commanders follow the "one-third—two-thirds rule" as a guide to allocate time available. They use one-third of the time available before execution for their planning and allocate the remaining two-thirds of the time available before execution to their subordinates for planning and preparation.

2-125. Both collaborative and parallel planning help optimize available planning time. *Collaborative planning is commanders, subordinate commanders, staffs, and other partners sharing information, knowledge, perceptions, ideas, and concepts regardless of physical location throughout the planning process.* Commanders, subordinate commanders, and staffs share their understanding of the situation and participate in course of action development and decisionmaking for development of the higher headquarters plan or order.

2-126. *Parallel planning is two or more echelons planning for the same operation sharing information sequentially through warning orders from the higher headquarters prior to the higher headquarters publishing their operation plan or operation order.* Since several echelons develop their plans simultaneously, parallel planning can significantly shorten planning time. The higher headquarters continuously shares information concerning future operations with subordinate units through warning orders and other means. Frequent communication between commanders and staffs and sharing of information (such as intelligence preparation of the battlefield products) help subordinate headquarters plan. Parallel planning requires significant interaction among echelons. During parallel planning, subordinate units do not wait for their higher headquarters to publish an order to begin developing their own plans and orders.

2-127. Higher commanders are sensitive not to overload subordinates with planning requirements. Generally, the higher the headquarters, the more time and staff resources are available to plan and explore options. Higher headquarters involve subordinates with developing those plans and concepts that have the highest likelihood of being adopted or fully developed.

PLANNING PITFALLS

2-128. Commanders and staffs recognize the value of planning and avoid common planning pitfalls. These pitfalls generally stem from a common cause: the failure to appreciate the unpredictability and uncertainty of military operations. Pointing these out is not a criticism of planning, but of planning improperly. The four pitfalls consist of—

- Attempting to forecast and dictate events too far into the future.
- Trying to plan in too much detail.
- Using the plan as a script for execution.
- Institutionalizing rigid planning methods.

2-129. The first pitfall, attempting to forecast and dictate events too far into the future, may result from believing a plan can control the future. Planners tend to plan based on assumptions that the future will be a linear continuation of the present. These plans often underestimate the scope of changes in directions that may occur and the results of second- and third-order effects. Even the most effective plans cannot anticipate all the unexpected events. Often, events overcome plans much sooner than anticipated. Effective plans include sufficient branches and sequels to account for the nonlinear nature of events.

2-130. The second pitfall consists of trying to plan in too much detail. Sound plans include necessary details; however, planning in unnecessary detail consumes limited time and resources that subordinates need. This pitfall often stems from the desire to leave as little as possible to chance. In general, the less certain the situation, the fewer details a plan should include. However, planners often respond to uncertainty by planning in more detail to try to account for every possibility. Preparing detailed plans under uncertain conditions generates even more anxiety, which leads to even more detailed planning. Often this over planning results in an extremely detailed plan that does not survive the friction of the situation and constricts effective action.

2-131. The third pitfall, using the plan as a script for execution, tries to prescribe the course of events with precision. When planners fail to recognize the limits of foresight and control, the plan can become a coercive and overly regulatory mechanism. Commanders, staffs, and subordinates mistakenly focus on meeting the requirements of the plan rather than deciding and acting effectively.

2-132. The fourth pitfall is the danger of institutionalizing rigid planning methods that leads to inflexible or overly structured thinking. This tends to make planning rigidly focused on the process and produces plans that overly emphasize detailed procedures. Effective planning provides a disciplined framework for approaching and solving complex problems. The danger is in taking that discipline to the extreme.

Chapter 3
Preparation

This chapter defines preparation and lists the preparation activities commonly performed within the headquarters and across the force to improve the unit's ability to execute operations. The chapter concludes by providing guidelines for effective preparation.

PREPARATION ACTIVITIES

3-1. *Preparation* consists of those activities performed by units and Soldiers to improve their ability to execute an operation (ADP 5-0). Preparation creates conditions that improve friendly forces' opportunities for success. It requires commander, staff, unit, and Soldier actions to ensure the force is trained, equipped, and ready to execute operations. Preparation activities help commanders, staffs, and Soldiers understand a situation and their roles in upcoming operations.

3-2. Mission success depends as much on preparation as on planning. Higher headquarters may develop the best of plans; however, plans serve little purpose if subordinates do not receive them in time. Subordinates need enough time to understand plans well enough to execute them. Subordinates develop their own plans and preparations for an operation. After they fully comprehend the plan, subordinate leaders rehearse key portions of it and ensure Soldiers and equipment are positioned and ready to execute the operation. Commanders, units, and Soldiers conduct the activities listed in table 3-1 to help ensure the force is protected and prepared for execution.

Table 3-1. Preparation activities

Continue to coordinate and conduct liaison	Conduct rehearsals
Initiate information collection	Conduct plans-to-operations transitions
Initiate security operations	Refine the plan
Initiate troop movement	Integrate new Soldiers and units
Initiate sustainment preparations	Complete task organization
Initiate network preparations	Train
Manage terrain	Perform pre-operations checks and inspections
Prepare terrain	Continue to build partnerships and teams
Conduct confirmation briefs	

CONTINUE TO COORDINATE AND CONDUCT LIAISON

3-3. Coordinating and conducting liaison helps ensure that leaders internal and external to the headquarters understand their unit's role in upcoming operations, and that they are prepared to perform that role. In addition to military forces, many civilian organizations may operate in the operational area. Their presence can both affect and be affected by the commander's operations. Continuous coordination and liaison between the command and unified action partners helps to build unity of effort.

3-4. During preparation, commanders continue to coordinate with higher, lower, adjacent, supporting, and supported units and civilian organizations. Coordination includes, but is not limited to the following:

- Sending and receiving liaison teams.
- Establishing communication links that ensure continuous contact during execution.
- Exchanging standard operating procedures (SOPs).
- Synchronizing security operations with reconnaissance and surveillance plans to prevent breaks in coverage.
- Facilitating civil-military coordination among those involved.

3-5. Establishing and maintaining liaison is vital to external coordination. Liaison enables direct communications between the sending and receiving headquarters. It may begin with planning and continue through preparing and executing, or it may start as late as execution. Available resources and the need for direct contact between sending and receiving headquarters determine when to establish liaison. Establishing liaisons with civilian organizations is especially important in stability operations because of the variety of external organizations and the inherent coordination challenges.

INITIATE INFORMATION COLLECTION

3-6. During preparation, commanders take every opportunity to improve their situational understanding prior to execution. This requires aggressive and continuous information collection. Commanders often direct information collection (to include reconnaissance operations) early in planning that continues in preparation and execution. Through information collection, commanders and staffs continuously plan, task, and employ collection assets and forces to collect timely and accurate information to help satisfy CCIRs and other information requirements (see FM 3-55).

INITIATE SECURITY OPERATIONS

3-7. The force as a whole is often most vulnerable to surprise and enemy attack during preparation, when forces are often concentrated in assembly areas. Leaders are away from their units and concentrated together during rehearsals. Parts of the force could be moving to task-organize. Required supplies may be unavailable or being repositioned. Security operations—screen, guard, cover, area security, and local security—are essential during preparation. Units assigned security missions execute these missions while the rest of the force prepares for the overall operation.

INITIATE TROOP MOVEMENTS

3-8. The repositioning of forces prior to execution is a significant activity of preparation. Commanders position or reposition units to the right starting places before execution. Commanders integrate operations security measures with troop movements to ensure these movements do not reveal any intentions to the enemy. Troop movements include assembly area reconnaissance by advance parties and route reconnaissance. They also include movements required by changes to the task organization. Commanders can use warning orders to direct troop movements before they issue the operation order.

INITIATE SUSTAINMENT PREPARATION

3-9. Resupplying, maintaining, and issuing supplies or equipment occurs during preparation. Any repositioning of sustainment assets can also occur. In addition, sustainment elements need to accomplish many other activities.

3-10. During preparation, sustainment planners at all levels take action to optimize means (force structure and resources) for supporting the commander's plan. These actions include, but are not limited to, identifying and preparing bases, host-nation infrastructure and capabilities, contract support requirements, and lines of communications. They also include forecasting and building operational stocks as well as identifying endemic health and environmental factors. Integrating environmental considerations will sustain vital resources and help reduce the logistics footprint.

3-11. Planners focus on identifying the resources currently available and ensuring access to them. During preparation, sustainment planning continues to support operational planning (branch and sequel development) and the targeting process.

INITIATE NETWORK PREPARATION

3-12. During preparation, the information network must be tailored and engineered to meet the specific needs of each operation. This includes not only the communications, but also how the commander expects information to move between and be available for leaders and units within an area of operations.

3-13. During preparation, commanders and staffs prepare and rehearse the information network to support the plan in the following areas:

- Management of available bandwidth.
- Availability and location of data and information.
- Positioning and structure of network assets.
- Tracking status of key network systems.
- Arraying sensors, weapons, and the information network to support the concept of the operation.

MANAGE TERRAIN

3-14. Terrain management is the process of allocating terrain by establishing areas of operation, designating assembly areas, and specifying locations for units and activities to deconflict other activities that might interfere with each other. Terrain management is an important activity during preparation as units reposition and stage prior to execution. Commanders assigned an area of operations manage terrain within their boundaries. Through terrain management, commanders identify and locate units in the area. The operations officer, with support from others in the staff, can then deconflict operations, control movements, and deter fratricide as units get in position to execute planned missions. Commanders also consider unified action partners located in their area of operations and coordinate with them for the use of terrain.

PREPARE TERRAIN

3-15. Terrain preparation starts with the situational understanding of terrain through proper terrain analysis. It involves shaping the terrain to gain an advantage, such as improving cover, concealment and observation, fields of fire, new obstacle effects through reinforcing obstacles, or mobility operations for initial positioning of forces. It can make the difference between the operation's success and failure. Commanders must understand the terrain and the infrastructure of their area of operations as early as possible to identify potential for improvement, establish priorities of work, and begin preparing the area.

CONDUCT CONFIRMATION BRIEFS

3-16. The confirmation brief is a key part of preparation. **A *confirmation brief* is a briefing subordinate leaders give to the higher commander immediately after the operation order is given. It is the leaders' understanding of the commander's intent, their specific tasks, and the relationship between their mission and the other units in the operation.** Subordinate leaders give a confirmation brief to the commander immediately after receiving the operation order. A confirmation brief ensures the commander that subordinate leaders understand—

- The commander's intent, mission, and concept of operations.
- Their unit's tasks and associated purposes.
- The relationship between their unit's mission and those of other units in the operation.

Ideally, the commander conducts confirmation briefs in person with selected staff members of the higher headquarters present.

CONDUCT REHEARSALS

3-17. **A *rehearsal* is a session in which the commander and staff or unit practices expected actions to improve performance during execution.** Commanders use this tool to ensure staffs and subordinates understand the concept of operations and commander's intent. Rehearsals also allow leaders to practice synchronizing operations at times and places critical to mission accomplishment. Effective rehearsals imprint a mental picture of the sequence of the operation's key actions and improve mutual understanding and coordination of subordinate and supporting leaders and units. The extent of rehearsals depends on available time. In cases of short-notice requirements, detailed rehearsals may not be possible. (See ATTP 5-0.1 for a discussion of the different types of rehearsals.)

CONDUCT PLANS-TO-OPERATIONS TRANSITION

3-18. The plans-to-operations transition is a preparation activity that occurs within the headquarters. It ensures members of the current operations cell fully understand the plan before execution. During preparation, the responsibility for developing and maintaining the plan shifts from the plans (or future operations) cell to the current operations cell (see figure 3-1). This transition is the point at which the current operations cell becomes responsible for controlling execution of the operation order. This responsibility includes answering requests for information concerning the order and maintaining the order through fragmentary orders. This transition enables the plans cell to focus its planning efforts on sequels, branches, and other planning requirements directed by the commander.

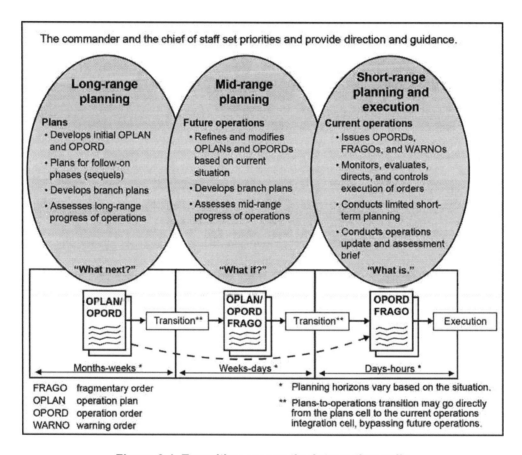

Figure 3-1. Transition among the integrating cells

3-19. The timing of the plans-to-operations transition requires careful consideration. It must allow enough time for members of the current operations cell to understand the plan well enough to coordinate and synchronize its execution. Ideally, the plans cell briefs the members of the current operations cell on the plans-to-operations transition before the combined arms rehearsal. This briefing enables members of the current operations cell to understand the upcoming operation as well as identify friction points and issues to solve prior to its execution. The transition briefing is a mission briefing that generally follows the five-paragraph operation order format. Specific areas addressed include, but are not limited to:

- Task organization.
- Situation.
- Higher headquarters' mission (one and two echelons up in the chain of command).

- Mission.
- Commander's intent (one and two echelons up in the chain of command).
- Concept of operations.
- Commander's critical information requirements.
- Decision support template and matrix.
- Branches and sequels.
- Sustainment.
- Command and signal.
- Outstanding requests for information and outstanding issues.

3-20. Following the combined arms rehearsal, planners and members of the current operations cell review additional planning guidance issued by the commander and modify the plan as necessary. Significant changes may require assistance from the plans cell to include moving a lead planner to the current operations cell. The plans cell continues planning for branches and sequels.

REVISE AND REFINE THE PLAN

3-21. Revising and refining the plan is a key activity of preparation. The commander's situational understanding may change over the course of operations, enemy actions may require revision of the plan, or unforeseen opportunities may arise. During preparation, assumptions made during planning may be proven true or false. Intelligence analysis may confirm or deny enemy actions or show changed conditions in the area of operations because of shaping operations. The status of friendly forces may change as the situation changes. In any of these cases, commanders identify the changed conditions and assess how the changes might affect the upcoming operation. Significant new information requires commanders to make one of three assessments regarding the plan:

- The new information validates the plan with no further changes.
- The new information requires adjustments to the plan.
- The new information invalidates the plan, requiring the commander to reframe and develop a new plan.

The earlier the commander identifies the need for adjustments, the more easily the staff can incorporate the changes to the plan and modify preparation activities.

COMPLETE TASK ORGANIZATION

3-22. During preparation, commanders complete task-organizing their force to obtain the right mix of capabilities and expertise to accomplish a specific mission. The receiving commander integrates units that are attached, placed under operational control, or placed in direct support. The commander directing the task organization also makes provisions for sustainment. The commander may direct task organization to occur immediately before the operation order is issued. This task-organizing is done with a warning order. Doing this gives units more time to execute the tasks needed to affect the new task organization. Task-organizing early allows affected units to become better integrated and more familiar with all elements involved. This is especially important with inherently time-consuming tasks, such as planning technical network support for the organization.

INTEGRATE NEW SOLDIERS AND UNITS

3-23. Commanders, command sergeants major, and staffs help assimilate new Soldiers into their units and new units into the force. They also prepare Soldiers and new units in performing their duties properly and integrating into an upcoming operation smoothly. Integration for new Soldiers includes training on unit SOPs and mission-essential tasks for the operation. It also means orienting new Soldiers on their places and roles in the force and during the operation. This integration for units includes, but is not limited to—

- Receiving and introducing new units to the force and the area of operations.
- Exchanging SOPs.
- Conducting briefings and rehearsals.

- Establishing communications links.
- Exchanging liaison teams (if required).

TRAIN

3-24. Training prepares forces and Soldiers to conduct operations according to doctrine, SOPs, and the unit's mission. Training develops the teamwork, trust, and mutual understanding that commanders need to exercise mission command and that forces need to achieve unity of effort. Training does not stop when a unit deploys. If the unit is not conducting operations or recovering from operations, it is training. While deployed, unit training focuses on fundamental skills, current SOPs, and skills for a specific mission.

CONDUCT PREOPERATIONS CHECKS AND INSPECTIONS

3-25. Unit preparation includes completing preoperations checks and inspections. These checks ensure Soldiers, units, and systems are as fully capable and ready to execute the mission as time and resources permit. The inspections ensure the force has the resources necessary to accomplish the mission. During preoperations checks and inspections, leaders also check Soldiers' ability to perform crew drills that may not be directly related to the mission. Some examples of these include drills that respond to a vehicle rollover or an onboard fire.

GUIDES TO EFFECTIVE PREPARATION

3-26. The following guidelines aid in effective preparation:
- Secure and protect the force.
- Improve situational understanding.
- Understand, rehearse, and refine the plan.
- Integrate, organize, and configure the force.
- Ensure forces and resources are ready and positioned.

SECURE AND PROTECT THE FORCE

3-27. The force as a whole is often most vulnerable to surprise and enemy attack during preparation. As such, security operations—screen, guard, cover, area security, and local security—are essential during preparation. In addition, commanders ensure integration of the various tasks of the protection warfighting function to safeguard bases, secure routes, and protect the force, while it prepares for operations.

IMPROVE SITUATIONAL UNDERSTANDING

3-28. During preparation, commanders may realize that the initial understanding they developed during planning may be neither accurate nor complete. As such, commanders strive to validate assumptions and improve their situational understanding, as they prepare for operations. Information collection (to include reconnaissance, surveillance, and intelligence operations) helps improve understanding of the enemy, terrain, and civil considerations. Inspections, rehearsals, liaison, and coordination help leaders improve their understanding of the friendly force.

UNDERSTAND, REFINE, AND REHEARSE THE PLAN

3-29. A successful transition from planning to execution requires those charged with executing the order to understand the plan fully. The transition between planning and execution takes place both internally in the headquarters and externally between the commander and subordinate commanders. Rehearsals, including confirmation briefings and the plans-to-operations transition briefing, help improve understanding of the concept of operations, control measures, decision points, and command and support relationships. Rehearsals are key events during preparation that assist the force with understanding the plan and practicing expected actions to improve performance during execution.

INTEGRATE, ORGANIZE, AND CONFIGURE THE FORCE

3-30. During preparation, commanders allocate time to put the new task organization into effect. This includes detaching units, moving forces, and receiving and integrating new units and Soldiers into the force. When units change task organization, they need preparation time to learn the gaining unit's standard operating procedures and the plan the gaining unit will execute. The gaining unit needs preparation time to assess the new unit's capabilities and limitations and to integrate new capabilities.

ENSURE FORCES AND RESOURCES ARE READY AND POSITIONED

3-31. Effective preparation ensures the right forces are in the right place, at the right time, with the right equipment and other resources ready to execute the operation. Concurrent with task organization, commanders use troop movement to position or reposition forces to the correct locations prior to execution. This includes positioning sustainment units and supplies.

Chapter 4

Execution

This chapter provides the guidelines for effective execution. It describes the role of the commander and staff in directing and controlling current operations. Next, this chapter describes decisionmaking in execution. The chapter concludes with a discussion of the rapid decisionmaking and synchronization process.

FUNDAMENTALS OF EXECUTION

4-1. *Execution* is putting a plan into action by applying combat power to accomplish the mission (ADP 5-0). In execution, commanders, staffs, and subordinate commanders focus their efforts on translating decisions into actions. They apply combat power to seize, retain, and exploit the initiative to gain and maintain a position of relative advantage. This is the essence of unified land operations.

4-2. Army forces seize, retain, and exploit the initiative through combined arms maneuver and wide area security. Through combined arms maneuver, commanders seize and exploit the initiative by forcing the enemy to respond to friendly action. Combined arms maneuver forces the enemy to react continuously until the enemy is finally driven into untenable positions. Seizing the initiative pressures enemy commanders into abandoning their preferred options and making costly mistakes. As enemy mistakes occur, friendly forces seize opportunities and create new avenues for exploitation. While combined arms maneuver is about seizing and exploiting the initiative, wide area security is about retaining the initiative. In wide area security, commanders focus combat power to protect populations, friendly forces, and infrastructure; to deny the enemy positions of advantage; and to consolidate gains to retain the initiative.

4-3. During execution, the situation may change rapidly. Operations the commander envisioned in the plan may bear little resemblance to actual events in execution. Subordinate commanders need maximum latitude to take advantage of situations and meet the higher commander's intent when the original order no longer applies. Effective execution requires leaders trained in independent decisionmaking, aggressiveness, and risk taking in an environment of mission command. During execution, leaders must be able and willing to solve problems within the commander's intent without constantly referring to higher headquarters. Subordinates need not wait for top-down synchronization to act. The following guides aid in effective execution:

- Seize the initiative through action.
- Accept prudent risk to exploit opportunities.

SEIZE THE INITIATIVE THROUGH ACTION

4-4. Commanders create conditions for seizing the initiative by acting. Without action, seizing the initiative is impossible. Faced with an uncertain situation, people naturally tend to hesitate and gather more information to reduce their uncertainty. However, waiting and gathering information might reduce uncertainty, but they will not eliminate it. Waiting may even increase uncertainty by providing the enemy with time to seize the initiative. It is far better to manage uncertainty by acting and developing the situation.

4-5. In operations dominated by stability tasks, commanders act quickly to improve the civil situation while preventing conditions from deteriorating further. Immediate action to stabilize the situation and provide for the immediate humanitarian needs of the people begins the process toward stability. Friendly forces dictate the terms of action and drive positive change to stabilize the situation rapidly. In turn, this improves the security environment, creating earlier opportunities for civilian agencies and organizations to contribute. By acting proactively to influence events, Army forces exploit the initiative to ensure steady progress toward conditions that support stability. Failing to act quickly may create a breeding ground for dissent and possible recruiting opportunities for enemies or adversaries.

ACCEPT PRUDENT RISK TO EXPLOIT OPPORTUNITIES

4-6.   Uncertainty and risk are inherent in all military operations. Successful commanders are comfortable operating under conditions of uncertainty, as they balance various risks and take advantage of opportunities. Opportunities are events that offer better ways to succeed. Commanders recognize opportunities by continuously monitoring and evaluating the situation. Failure to understand the opportunities inherent in an enemy's action surrenders the initiative. Most opportunities are fleeting. When they present themselves, commanders usually have only a short window of time in which to act. In operations, it is better to err on the side of speed, audacity, and momentum than on the side of caution, all else being equal. Bold decisions give the best promise of success; however, when acting on an opportunity, commanders must consider the difference between a prudent risk and a gamble.

4-7.   *Prudent risk* is a deliberate exposure to potential injury or loss when the commander judges the outcome in terms of mission accomplishment as worth the cost (ADP 6-0). Reasonably estimating and intentionally accepting risk is not gambling. Gambling, in contrast to prudent risk taking, is staking the success of an entire action on a single event without considering the hazard to the force should the event not unfold as envisioned. Therefore, commanders avoid taking gambles. Commanders carefully determine risks, analyze and minimize as many hazards as possible, and then take prudent risks to exploit opportunities.

4-8.   Because uncertainty exists in all military operations, every military decision contains risk. Commanders exercise the art of command when deciding how much risk to accept. As shown in figure 4-1, the commander has several techniques available to reduce the risk associated in a specific operation. Some of these techniques for reducing risk take resources from the decisive operation, which reduces the concentration of effects at the decisive point.

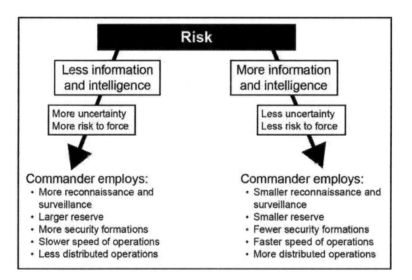

Figure 4-1. Risk reduction factors

4-9.   The commander has the option to redirect the efforts of forces previously used to reduce risk toward strengthening the force's decisive operation as more information becomes available. In any operation, the relationship between information, uncertainty, risk, size of reserves and security forces, and the disposition of the main body may change frequently. The commander must continually weigh this balance and make adjustments as needed.

4-10. These adjustments can create problems. Too many changes or changes made too rapidly in task organization, mission, and priorities can have negative effects on the operations process. For example, if a commander changes task organization too frequently, the force fails to develop the flexibility provided by teamwork. On the other hand, if the commander fails to change the task organization when dictated by circumstances, the force lacks flexibility to adapt to those changing circumstances. It is then unable to react effectively to enemy moves or act with the concentration of effects that lead to mission success. (See FM 3-90 for a detailed discussion of the art of tactics and risk reduction.)

RESPONSIBILITIES DURING EXECUTION

4-11. During execution, commanders focus their activities on directing, assessing, and leading while improving their understanding and modifying their visualization. Initially, commanders direct the transition from planning to execution as the order is issued and the responsibility for integration passes from the plans cell to the current operations integration cell. During execution, the staff directs units, within delegated authority, to keep the operation progressing successfully. Assessing allows the commander and staff to determine the existence and significance of variances from the operations as envisioned in the initial plan. The staff makes recommendations to the commander about what action to take concerning identified variances in the plan. During execution, leading is as important as decisionmaking, as commanders influence subordinates by providing purpose, direction, and motivation.

COMMANDERS, DEPUTIES, AND COMMAND SERGEANTS MAJOR

4-12. During execution, commanders at all levels locate themselves where they can exercise command and sense the operation. Sometimes this is at the command post. At other times, commanders may use the command group or mobile command post to command from a forward location. Commanders balance the need to make personal observations, provide command presence, and sense the mood of subordinates from a forward location with the ability to maintain communication and control with the entire force from a command post. No matter where they are located, commanders are always looking beyond the current operation to anticipate future actions. They must periodically step back from the current situation and look at how the force is positioning itself for future operations.

4-13. Deputy commanders provide a command resource during execution. First, they can serve as senior advisors to their commander. Second, deputy commanders may directly supervise a specific warfighting function (for example, sustainment). Finally, deputy commanders can command a specific operation (such as a gap crossing), area, or part of the unit (such as the covering force) for the commander.

4-14. The command sergeant major provides another set of senior eyes to assist the commander. The command sergeant major assists the commander with assessing operations as well as assessing the condition and morale of forces. In addition, the command sergeant major provides leadership and expertise to units and Soldiers at critical locations and times during execution.

STAFF

4-15. The chief of staff (COS) or executive officer (XO) integrates the efforts of the whole staff during execution. These efforts include the assignment of responsibilities among staff sections and command post cells for conducting analysis and decisionmaking. While the unit standard operating procedures might specify a division of responsibilities among integrating cells for these matters, often the COS (XO) makes specific decisions allocating responsibilities among cells.

4-16. In execution, the staff—primarily through the current operations integration cell—integrates forces and warfighting functions to accomplish the mission. The staff assesses short-term actions and activities as part of this integration. While the COS (XO) integrates staff activities among all functional and integrating cells and separate sections, the operations officer integrates the operation through the current operations integration cell. Other staff principals integrate within their areas of expertise.

4-17. Formal and informal integration of the warfighting functions by functional and integrating cells is continuous. Informal integration occurs both within and among command post cells and staff sections and between headquarters. When staffs need a more structured (formal) integration, they establish meetings (to include working groups and boards) to share information, coordinate actions, and solve problems. The COS (XO) also identifies staff members to participate in the higher commander's working groups and boards.

4-18. The current operations integration cell is the integrating cell in the command post with primary responsibility for execution. Staff members in the current operations integration cell actively assist the commander and subordinate units in controlling the current operation. They provide information, synchronize staff and subordinate unit or echelon activities, and coordinate support requests from subordinates. The current operations integration cell solves problems and acts within the authority delegated by the commander. It also performs some short-range planning using the rapid decisionmaking and synchronization process. (See paragraphs 4-30 through 4-47.)

4-19. Several decision support tools assist the commander and staff during execution. Among the most important are the decision support template, decision support matrix, and execution matrix. The current operations integration cell uses these tools, among others, to help control operations and to determine when anticipated decisions are coming up for execution.

4-20. A *decision support template* is a combined intelligence and operations graphic based on the results of wargaming. The decision support template depicts decision points, timelines associated with movement of forces and the flow of the operation, and other key items of information required to execute a specific friendly course of action (JP 2-01.3). Part of the decision support template is the decision support matrix. **A *decision support matrix* is a written record of a war-gamed course of action that describes decision points and associated actions at those decision points**. The decision support matrix lists decision points, locations of decision points, criteria to be evaluated at decision points, actions that occur at decision points, and the units responsible to act on the decision points. It also lists the units responsible for observing and reporting information affecting the criteria for decisions.

4-21. **An *execution matrix* is a visual and sequential representation of the critical tasks and responsible organizations by time**. An execution matrix could be for the entire force, such as an air assault execution matrix, or it may be specific to a warfighting function, such as a fire support execution matrix. The current operations integration cell uses the execution matrix to determine which friendly actions to expect forces to execute in the near term or, in conjunction with the decision support matrix, which execution decisions to make.

DECISIONMAKING DURING EXECUTION

4-22. Decisionmaking is tied to disciplined initiative and is inherent in executing operations. Commanders observe the progress of operations and intervene when necessary to ensure success. Because operations never unfold exactly as envisioned and because understanding of the situation changes, a commander's decisions made during execution are critical to an operation's success. During execution, commanders direct their units forcefully and promptly to overcome the difficulties of enemy action, friendly failures, errors, and other changes in their operational environment.

4-23. Commanders make execution and adjustment decisions throughout execution. Execution decisions implement a planned action under circumstances anticipated in the order. An execution decision is normally tied to a *decision point*—a point in space or time the commander or staff anticipate making a key decision concerning a specific course of action (JP 5-0). An adjustment decision is the selection of a course of action that modifies the order to respond to unanticipated opportunities or threats. An adjustment decision may include a decision to reframe the problem and develop an entirely new plan.

4-24. Executing, adjusting, or abandoning the original operation is part of decisionmaking in execution. By fighting the enemy and not the plan, successful commanders balance the tendency to abandon a well-conceived plan too soon against persisting in a failing effort too long. Effective decisionmaking during execution—

- Relates all actions to the commander's intent and concept of operations to ensure they support the decisive operation.
- Is comprehensive, maintaining integration of combined arms rather than dealing with separate functions.
- Relies heavily on intuitive decisionmaking by commanders and staffs to make rapid adjustments.
- Is continuous and responds effectively to any opportunity or threat.

ASSESSMENT AND DECISIONMAKING

4-25. As commanders assess an operation, they determine when decisions are required. Plans usually identify some decision points; however, unexpected enemy actions or other changes often present situations that require unanticipated decisions. Commanders act when these decisions are required; they do not wait for a set time in the battle rhythm. As commanders assess the operation, they describe their impressions to the staff and subordinates and discuss the desirability of choices available. Once commanders make decisions, their staffs transmit the necessary directives.

4-26. Assessment in execution identifies variances, their magnitude and significance, and the need for and types of decisions—whether execution or adjustment—to be made. (See chapter 5 for a detailed discussion of assessment.) The commander and staff assess the probable outcome of the operation to determine whether changes are necessary to accomplish the mission, take advantage of opportunities, or react to unexpected threats. Figure 4-2 depicts a basic model of assessing and decisionmaking during execution.

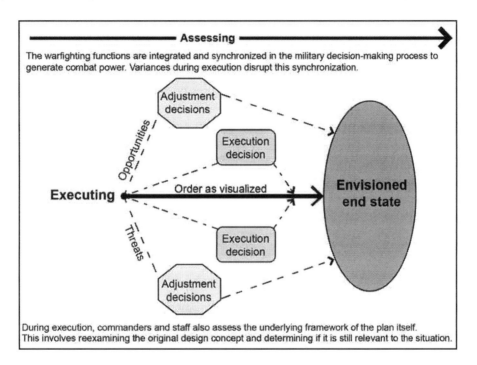

Figure 4-2. Decisions in execution

Variances

4-27. A variance is a difference between the actual situation during an operation and what the plan forecasted the situation would be at that time or event. Staffs ensure information systems display relevant information that allows them to identify variances. The commander and staff evaluate emerging variances. If necessary, staffs update the conclusions and recommendations of their running estimates for the commander, who directs the necessary action. Two forms of variances exist: opportunities and threats.

4-28. The first form of variance is an opportunity to accomplish the mission more effectively. Opportunity results from forecasted or unexpected success. When commanders recognize an opportunity, they alter the order to exploit it if the change achieves the end state without incurring unacceptable risk. When exploiting an opportunity, the concept of operations may change, but the commander's intent usually remains the same.

4-29. The second form of variance is a threat to mission accomplishment or survival of the force. When recognizing a threat, the commander adjusts the order to eliminate the enemy advantage, restore the friendly advantage, and regain the initiative. Not all threats to the force or mission involve hostile or neutral persons. Disease, toxic hazards, and natural disasters are examples of other threats.

4-30. In some instances, the variance is so extreme that no branch or sequel is available or the current plan lacks enough flexibility to respond to the variance. In this situation, the commander and staff may have to reframe the operational environment and the problem resulting in a new plan, as shown in figure 4-2 on page 4-3. (See chapter 3 for a more detailed discussion of reframing and assessment.)

Types of Decisions

4-31. Decisions made during execution are either execution decisions or adjustment decisions. Execution decisions involve options anticipated in the order. Adjustment decisions involve options that commanders did not anticipate. These decisions may include a decision to reframe the problem and develop an entirely new plan. Commanders may delegate authority for some execution decisions to the staff; however, commanders are always responsible for and involved in decisions during execution.

4-32. Execution decisions implement a planned action under circumstances anticipated in the order. In their most basic form, execution decisions are decisions the commander foresees and identifies for execution during the operation. They apply resources at times or situations already established in the order. For example, changing a boundary, altering the task organization, transitioning between phases, and executing a branch are execution decisions. Commanders are responsible for those decisions but may direct the COS (XO) or staff officer to supervise implementation. The current operations integration cell oversees the synchronization of integrating processes needed to implement execution decisions.

4-33. Adjustment decisions modify the operation to respond to unanticipated opportunities and threats. They often require implementing unanticipated operations and resynchronizing the warfighting functions. Commanders make these decisions, delegating implementing authority only after directing the major change themselves.

RAPID DECISIONMAKING AND SYNCHRONIZATION PROCESS

4-34. The rapid decisionmaking and synchronization process (RDSP) is a decisionmaking and synchronization technique that commanders and staffs commonly use during execution. While identified here with a specific name and method, the approach is not new; its use in the Army is well established. Commanders and staffs develop this capability through training and practice. The RDSP includes five steps. The first two may be performed in any order, including concurrently. The last three are performed interactively until commanders identify an acceptable course of action. (See figure 4-3.)

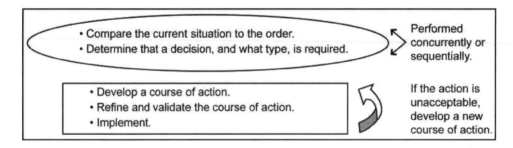

Figure 4-3. Rapid decisionmaking and synchronization process

4-35. While the military decisionmaking process (MDMP) seeks the optimal solution, the RDSP seeks a timely and effective solution within the commander's intent, mission, and concept of operations. Using the RDSP lets leaders avoid the time-consuming requirements of developing decision criteria and comparing courses of action (COAs). Operational and mission variables continually change during execution. This often invalidates or weakens COAs and decision criteria before leaders can make a decision. Under the RDSP, leaders combine their experience and intuition to quickly reach situational understanding. Based on this, they develop and refine workable COAs.

COMPARE THE CURRENT SITUATION TO THE ORDER

4-36. During execution, commanders and staffs monitor the situation to identify changes in conditions. Then they ask if these changes affect the overall conduct of operations or their part of it and if the changes are significant. Finally, they identify if the changed conditions represent variances from the order—especially opportunities and risks. Staff members use running estimates to look for indicators of variances that affect their areas of expertise. The commander, COS (XO), and command post cell chiefs look for indicators of variances that affect the overall operation.

4-37. Staff members are particularly alert for answers to CCIRs that support anticipated decisions. They also watch for exceptional information. Exceptional information is information that would have answered one of the commander's critical information requirements if the requirement for it had been foreseen and stated as one of the commander's critical information requirements.

DETERMINE THE TYPE OF DECISION REQUIRED

4-38. When a variance is identified, the commander directs action while the chief of operations leads chiefs of the current operations integration cell and selected functional cells in quickly comparing the current situation to the expected situation. This assessment accomplishes the following:

- Describes the variance.
- Determines if the variance provides a significant opportunity or threat and examines the potential of either.
- Determines if a decision is needed by identifying if the variance:
  - Indicates an opportunity that can be exploited to accomplish the mission faster or with fewer resources.
  - Directly threatens the decisive operation's success.
  - Threatens a shaping operation such that it may threaten the decisive operation directly or in the near future.
  - Can be addressed within the commander's intent and concept of operations. (If so, determine what execution decision is needed.)
  - Requires changing the concept of operations substantially. (If so, determine what adjustment decision or new approach will best suit the circumstances.)

4-39. For minor variances, the chief of operations works with other cell chiefs to determine whether changes to control measures are needed. If so, they determine how those changes affect other warfighting functions. They direct changes within their authority (execution decisions) and notify the COS (XO) and the affected command post cells and staff elements.

4-40. Commanders intervene directly in cases that affect the overall direction of the unit. They describe the situation, direct their subordinates to provide any additional information they need, and order either implementation of planned responses or development of an order to redirect the force.

DEVELOP A COURSE OF ACTION

4-41. If the variance requires an adjustment decision, the designated integrating cell and affected command post cell chiefs recommend implementation of a COA or obtain the commander's guidance for developing one. They use the following conditions to screen possible COAs:

- Mission.
- Commander's intent.
- Current dispositions and freedom of action.
- CCIRs.
- Limiting factors, such as supply constraints, boundaries, and combat strength.

4-42. The new options must conform to the commander's intent. Possible COAs may alter the concept of operations and CCIRs, if they remain within the commander's intent. However, the commander approves changes to the CCIRs. Functional cell chiefs and other staff section leaders identify areas that may be affected within their areas of expertise by proposed changes to the order or mission. The commander is as likely as anyone else to detect the need for change and to sketch out the options. Whether the commander, COS (XO), or chief of operations does this, the future operations cell is often directed to further develop the concept and draft the order. The chief of operations and the current operations integration cell normally lead this effort, especially if the response is needed promptly or the situation is not complex. The commander or COS (XO) is usually the decisionmaking authority, depending on the commander's delegation of authority.

4-43. Commanders may delegate authority for execution decisions to their deputies, COSs (XOs), or their operations officers. They retain personal responsibility for all decisions and normally retain the authority for approving adjustment decisions.

4-44. When reallocating resources or priorities, commanders assign only minimum essential assets to shaping operations. They use all other assets to weight the decisive operation. This applies when allocating resources for the overall operation or within a warfighting function.

4-45. Commanders normally direct the future operations cell or the current operations integration cell to prepare a fragmentary order setting conditions for executing a new COA. When lacking time to perform the MDMP or quickness of action is desirable, commanders make an immediate adjustment decision—using intuitive decisionmaking—in the form of a focused COA. Developing the focused COA often follows mental war-gaming by commanders until they reach an acceptable COA. If time is available, commanders may direct the plans cell to develop a new COA using the MDMP, and the considerations for planning become operative.

REFINE AND VALIDATE THE COURSE OF ACTION

4-46. Once commanders describe the new COA, the current operations integration cell conducts an analysis to validate its feasibility, suitability, and acceptability. If acceptable, the COA is refined to resynchronize the warfighting functions enough to generate and apply the needed combat power. Staffs with a future operations cell may assign that cell responsibility for developing the details of the new COA and drafting a fragmentary order to implement it. The commander or COS (XO) may direct an "on-call" operations synchronization meeting to perform this task and ensure rapid resynchronization.

4-47. Validation and refinement are done quickly. Normally, the commander and staff officers conduct a mental war game of the new COA. They consider potential enemy reactions, the unit's counteractions, and secondary effects that might affect the force's synchronization. Each staff member considers the following items:

- Is the new COA feasible in terms of my area of expertise?
- How will this action affect my area of expertise?
- Does it require changing my information requirements?
  - Should any of the information requirements be nominated as a CCIR?
  - What actions within my area of expertise does this change require?
  - Will this COA require changing objectives or targets nominated by the staff section?
- What other command post cells and elements does this action affect?
- What are potential enemy reactions?
- What are the possible friendly counteractions?
  - Does this counteraction affect my area of expertise?
  - Will it require changing my information requirements?
  - Are any of my information requirements potential CCIRs?
  - What actions within my area of expertise does this counteraction require?
  - Will it require changing objectives or targets nominated by the staff section?
  - What other command post cells and elements does this counteraction affect?

4-48. The validation and refinement will show if the COA will acceptably solve the problem. If it does not, the COS or chief of operations modifies it through additional analysis or develops a new COA. The COS (XO) informs the commander of any changes made to the COA.

IMPLEMENT

4-49. When a COA is acceptable, the COS (XO) recommends implementation to the commander or implements it directly, if the commander has delegated that authority. Implementation normally requires a fragmentary order; in exceptional circumstances, it may require a new operation order. That order changes the concept of operations (in adjustment decisions), resynchronizes the warfighting functions, and disseminates changes to control measures. The staff uses warning orders to alert subordinates to a pending change. The staff also establishes sufficient time for the unit to implement the change without losing integration or being exposed to unnecessary tactical risk.

4-50. Commanders often issue orders to subordinates verbally in situations requiring quick reactions. At battalion and higher levels, written fragmentary orders confirm verbal orders to ensure synchronization, integration, and notification of all parts of the force. If time permits, leaders verify that subordinates understand critical tasks. Methods for doing this include the confirmation brief and backbrief. These are conducted both between commanders and within staff elements to ensure mutual understanding.

4-51. After the analysis is complete, the current operations integration cell and command post cell chiefs update decision support templates and synchronization matrixes. When time is available, the operations officer or chief of operations continues this analysis to the operation's end to complete combat power integration. Staff members begin the synchronization needed to implement the decision. This synchronization involves collaboration with other command post cells and subordinate staffs. Staff members determine how actions in their areas of expertise affect others. They coordinate those actions to eliminate undesired effects that might cause friction. The cells provide results of this synchronization to the current operations integration cell and the common operational picture.

Chapter 5

Assessment

This chapter defines assessment and describes its purpose. Next, it describes an assessment process and offers fundamentals commanders and staffs consider for effective assessment. This chapter concludes with a discussion of assessment working groups and assessment support from operations research and systems analysis. (See ATTP 5-01.1 for doctrine on developing assessment plans.)

ASSESSMENT AND THE OPERATIONS PROCESS

5-1. *Assessment* is the determination of the progress toward accomplishing a task, creating an effect, or achieving an objective (JP 3-0). Assessment precedes and guides the other activities of the operations process. Assessment involves deliberately comparing forecasted outcomes with actual events to determine the overall effectiveness of force employment. More specifically, assessment helps the commander determine progress toward attaining the desired end state, achieving objectives, and performing tasks. It also involves continuously monitoring and evaluating the operational environment to determine what changes might affect the conduct of operations.

5-2. Throughout the operations process, commanders integrate their own assessments with those of the staff, subordinate commanders, and other unified action partners. Primary tools for assessing progress of the operation include the operation order, the common operational picture, personal observations, running estimates, and the assessment plan. The latter includes measures of effectiveness, measures of performance, and reframing criteria. The commander's visualization forms the basis for the commander's personal assessment of progress. Running estimates provide information, conclusions, and recommendations from the perspective of each staff section.

THE ASSESSMENT PROCESS

5-3. Assessment is continuous; it precedes and guides every operations process activity and concludes each operation or phase of an operation. Broadly, assessment consists of, but is not limited to, the following activities:

- Monitoring the current situation to collect relevant information.
- Evaluating progress toward attaining end state conditions, achieving objectives, and performing tasks.
- Recommending or directing action for improvement.

MONITORING

5-4. *Monitoring* **is continuous observation of those conditions relevant to the current operation.** Monitoring within the assessment process allows staffs to collect relevant information, specifically that information about the current situation that can be compared to the forecasted situation described in the commander's intent and concept of operations. Progress cannot be judged, nor effective decisions made, without an accurate understanding of the current situation.

5-5. During planning, commanders monitor the situation to develop facts and assumptions that underlie the plan. During preparation and execution, commanders and staffs monitor the situation to determine if the facts are still relevant, if their assumptions remain valid, and if new conditions emerged that affect the operations.

5-6. Commander's critical information requirements and decision points focus the staff's monitoring activities and prioritize the unit's collection efforts. Information requirements concerning the enemy, terrain and weather, and civil considerations are identified and assigned priorities through reconnaissance and surveillance. Operations officers use friendly reports to coordinate other assessment-related information requirements. To prevent duplicated collection efforts, information requirements associated with assessing the operation are integrated into both the reconnaissance and surveillance plan and friendly force information requirements.

5-7. Staffs monitor and collect information from the common operational picture and friendly reports. This information includes operational and intelligence summaries from subordinate, higher, and adjacent headquarters and communications and reports from liaison teams. Staffs also identify information sources outside military channels and monitor their reports. These other channels might include products from civilian, host-nation, and other government agencies. Staffs apply information management and knowledge management to facilitate getting this information to the right people at the right time.

5-8. Staff sections record relevant information in running estimates. Staff sections maintain a continuous assessment of current operations as a basis to determine if they are proceeding according to the commander's intent, mission, and concept of operations. In their running estimates, staff sections use this new information and these updated facts and assumptions as the basis for evaluation.

EVALUATING

5-9. The staff analyzes relevant information collected through monitoring to evaluate the operation's progress. *Evaluating* **is using criteria to judge progress toward desired conditions and determining why the current degree of progress exists.** Evaluation is at the heart of the assessment process where most of the analysis occurs. Evaluation helps commanders determine what is working and what is not working, and it helps them gain insights into how to better accomplish the mission.

5-10. Criteria in the forms of measures of effectiveness (MOEs) and measures of performance (MOPs) aid in determining progress toward attaining end state conditions, achieving objectives, and performing tasks. MOEs help determine if a task is achieving its intended results. MOPs help determine if a task is completed properly. MOEs and MOPs are simply criteria—they do not represent the assessment itself. MOEs and MOPs require relevant information in the form of indicators for evaluation.

5-11. A *measure of effectiveness* is a criterion used to assess changes in system behavior, capability, or operational environment that is tied to measuring the attainment of an end state, achievement of an objective, or creation of an effect (JP 3-0). MOEs help measure changes in conditions, both positive and negative. MOEs help to answer the question "Are we doing the right things?" MOEs are commonly found and tracked in formal assessment plans. Examples of MOEs for the objective to "Provide a safe and secure environment" may include:

- Decrease in insurgent activity.
- Increase in population trust of host-nation security forces.

5-12. A *measure of performance* is a criterion used to assess friendly actions that is tied to measuring task accomplishment (JP 3-0). MOPs help answer questions such as "Was the action taken?" or "Were the tasks completed to standard?" A MOP confirms or denies that a task has been properly performed. MOPs are commonly found and tracked at all levels in execution matrixes. MOPs are also commonly used to evaluate training. MOPs help to answer the question "Are we doing things right?"

5-13. At the most basic level, every Soldier assigned a task maintains a formal or informal checklist to track task completion. The status of those tasks and subtasks are MOPs. Similarly, operations consist of a series of collective tasks sequenced in time, space, and purpose to accomplish missions. Current operations integration cells use MOPs in execution matrixes and running estimates to track completed tasks. The uses of MOPs are a primary element of battle tracking. MOPs focus on the friendly force. Evaluating task accomplishment using MOPs is relatively straightforward and often results in a yes or no answer. Examples of MOPs include—

- Route X cleared.
- Generators delivered, are operational, and are secured at villages A, B, and C.

- Hill 785 secured.
- Aerial dissemination of 10,000 leaflets over village D.

5-14. In the context of assessment, an *indicator* is **an item of information that provides insight into a measure of effectiveness or measure of performance**. Indicators take the form of reports from subordinates, surveys and polls, and information requirements. Indicators help to answer the question "What is the current status of this MOE or MOP?" A single indicator can inform multiple MOPs and MOEs. Examples of indicators for the MOE "Decrease in insurgent activity" are:

- Number of hostile actions per area each week.
- Number of munitions caches found per area each week.
- Number of reports of insurgent activity by the population per area per week.

Table 5-1 provides additional information concerning MOEs, MOPs, and indicators.

Table 5-1. Assessment measures and indicators

MOE	MOP	Indicator
Answers the question: Are we doing the right things?	Answers the question: Are we doing things right?	Answers the question: What is the status of this MOE or MOP?
Measures purpose accomplishment.	Measures task completion.	Measures raw data inputs to inform MOEs and MOPs.
Measures *why* in the mission statement.	Measures *what* in the mission statement.	Information used to make measuring what or why possible.
No hierarchical relationship to MOPs.	No hierarchical relationship to MOEs.	Subordinate to MOEs and MOPs.
Often formally tracked in formal assessment plans.	Often formally tracked in execution matrixes.	Often formally tracked in formal assessment plans.
Typically challenging to choose the correct ones.	Typically simple to choose the correct ones.	Typically as challenging to select correctly as the supported MOE or MOP.

5-15. Evaluation includes analysis of why progress is or is not being made according to the plan. Commanders and staffs propose and consider possible causes. In particular, the question of whether or not changes in the situation can be attributed to friendly actions is addressed. Commanders and staffs consult subject matter experts, both internal and external to the staff, on whether staffs have identified the correct underlying causes for specific changes in the situation. Assumptions identified in the planning process are challenged to determine if they are still valid.

5-16. A key aspect of evaluation is determining variances—the difference between the actual situation and what the plan forecasted the situation would be at the time or event. Based on the significance of the variances, the staff makes recommendations to the commander on how to adjust operations to accomplish the mission more effectively. (See chapter 4 for a detailed discussion of assessment during execution to include the relationship between the degree of variance from the plan and execution and adjustment decisions.)

5-17. Evaluating includes considering whether the desired conditions have changed, are no longer achievable, or are not achievable through the current operational approach. This is done by continually challenging the key assumptions made when framing the problem. When an assumption is invalidated, then reframing may be in order.

RECOMMENDING OR DIRECTING ACTION

5-18. Monitoring and evaluating are critical activities; however, assessment is incomplete without recommending or directing action. Assessment may diagnose problems, but unless it results in recommended adjustments, its use to the commander is limited.

5-19. Based on the evaluation of progress, the staff brainstorms possible improvements to the plan and makes preliminary judgments about the relative merit of those changes. Staff members identify those changes possessing sufficient merit and provide them as recommendations to the commander or make adjustments within their delegated authority. Recommendations to the commander range from continuing the operation as planned, to executing a branch, or to making unanticipated adjustments. Making adjustments includes assigning new tasks to subordinates, reprioritizing support, adjusting information collection assets, and significantly modifying the course of action. Commanders integrate recommendations from the staff, subordinate commanders, and other partners with their personal assessment. Using those recommendations, they decide if and how to modify the operation to better accomplish the mission.

5-20. Assessment diagnoses threats, suggests improvements to effectiveness, and reveals opportunities. The staff presents the results and conclusions of its assessments and recommendations to the commander as an operation develops. Just as the staff devotes time to analysis and evaluation, so too must it make timely, complete, and actionable recommendations. The chief of staff or executive officer ensures the staff completes its analyses and recommendations in time to affect the operation and for information to reach the commander when needed.

5-21. When developing recommendations, the staff draws from many sources and considers its recommendations within the larger context of the operations. While several ways to improve a particular aspect of the operation might exist, some recommendations could impact other aspects of the operation. As with all recommendations, the staff should address any future implications.

GUIDES TO EFFECTIVE ASSESSMENT

5-22.   Throughout the conduct of operations, commanders integrate their own assessments with those of the staff, subordinate commanders, and other partners in the area of operations. The following guides aid in effective assessment:

- Commanders prioritize the assessment effort.
- Incorporate the logic of the plan.
- Use caution when establishing cause and effect.
- Combine quantitative and qualitative indicators.

COMMANDERS PRIORITIZE THE ASSESSMENT EFFORT

5-23. Commanders establish priorities for assessment in their planning guidance, CCIRs, and decision points. By prioritizing the effort, commanders avoid excessive analyses when assessing operations. Committing valuable time and energy to developing excessive and time-consuming assessment schemes squanders resources better devoted to other operations process activities. Commanders reject the tendency to measure something just because it is measurable. Effective commanders avoid burdening subordinates and staffs with overly detailed assessments and collection tasks. Generally, the echelon at which a specific operation, task, or action is conducted should be the echelon at which it is assessed.

INCORPORATE THE LOGIC OF THE PLAN

5-24. Effective assessment relies on an accurate understanding of the logic (reasoning) used to build the plan. Each plan is built on assumptions and an operational approach. The reasons or logic as to why the commander believes the plan will produce the desired results are important considerations when staffs determine how to assess operations. Recording and understanding this logic helps the staffs recommend the appropriate measures of effectiveness, measures of performance, and indicators for assessing the operation.

USE CAUTION WHEN ESTABLISHING CAUSE AND EFFECT

5-25. Although establishing cause and effect is sometimes difficult, it is crucial to effective assessment. Sometimes, establishing causality between actions and their effects can be relatively straightforward, such as in observing a bomb destroy a bridge. In other instances, especially regarding changes in human behavior, attitudes, and perception, establishing links between cause and effect proves difficult. Commanders and staffs must guard against drawing erroneous conclusions in these instances.

COMBINE QUANTITATIVE AND QUALITATIVE INDICATORS

5-26. Effective assessment incorporates both quantitative (observation-based) and qualitative (opinion-based) indicators. Human judgment is integral to assessment. A key aspect of any assessment is the degree to which it relies upon human judgment and the degree to which it relies upon direct observation and mathematical rigor. Rigor offsets the inevitable bias, while human judgment focuses rigor and processes on intangibles that are often key to success. The appropriate balance depends on the situation—particularly the nature of the operation and available resources for assessment—but rarely lies at the ends of the scale.

ASSESSMENT WORKING GROUPS

5-27. Assessing progress is the responsibility of all staff sections and not the purview of any one staff section or command post cell. Each staff section assesses the operation from its specific area of expertise. However, these staff sections must coordinate and integrate their individual assessments and associated recommendations across the warfighting functions to produce comprehensive assessments for the commander, particularly in protracted operations. They do this in the assessment working group.

5-28. Assessment working groups are more common at higher echelons (division and above) and are more likely to be required in protracted operations. Normally, the frequency of meetings is part of a unit's battle rhythm. The staff, however, does not wait for a scheduled working group to inform the commander on issues that require immediate attention. Nor do they wait to take action in those areas within their delegated authority.

5-29. The assessment working group is cross-functional by design and includes membership from across the staff, liaison personnel, and other unified action partners outside the headquarters. Commanders direct the chief of staff, executive officer, or a staff section leader to run the assessment working group. Typically, the operations officer, plans officer, or senior operations research/systems analysis (ORSA) staff section serves as the staff lead for the assessment working group.

5-30. Minority views are heard and dissenters speak up in the assessment working group. Commanders encourage all subject matter experts and relevant staff sections to debate vigorously on the proper understanding of observed trends and their associated causes. Minority views often create critical insights; they are also presented to the commander at the assessment board.

5-31. The frequency with which the assessment working group meets depends on the situation. Additionally, the assessment working group may present its findings and recommendations to the commander for decision. Subordinate commanders may participate and provide their assessments of the operations and recommendations along with the staff. Commanders combine these assessments with their personal assessment, consider recommendations, and then direct changes to improve performance and better accomplish the mission.

ASSESSMENT SUPPORT

5-32. The ORSA staff section supports assessment on many levels. Staff analytical resources and expertise increase at each echelon. Division and corps headquarters, for example, have an assigned ORSA staff section. In addition to managing a formal assessment framework, these staff sections can provide other capabilities to assist the commander. These capabilities include trend analysis, hypothesis testing, and forecasting.

5-33. ORSA staff sections use various mathematical techniques to identify and analyze trends in data. They confirm or rule out suspected trends in a statistically rigorous manner. They can also determine how much a given trend depends on other variables within the information. For example, given sufficient information, the ORSA staff section can determine which essential services trends correlate most to the trend in the number of attacks.

5-34. The ORSA staff section confirms or rules out many theories about given information. For example, the commander may propose a hypothesis that enemy surface-to-air attacks increased because helicopter flight patterns became too predictable. The ORSA cell can analyze the flight patterns and determine a correlation to attacks to confirm or rule out the hypothesis.

5-35. The ORSA staff section can use statistical techniques to predict the next information point in a series. Margins of error for this activity can be significant, but it is one more tool the commander can use to develop estimates in an unknown situation.

Glossary

The glossary lists acronyms and terms with Army or joint definitions. Where Army and Joint definitions differ, (Army) precedes the definition. Terms for which ADRP 5-0 is the proponent are marked with an asterisk (*). The proponent publication for other terms is listed in parentheses after the definition.

SECTION I – ACRONYMS AND ABBREVIATIONS

ADCON	administrative control
ADP	Army doctrine publication
ADRP	Army doctrine reference publication
ATTP	Army tactics, techniques, and procedures
ASCOPE	areas, structures, capabilities, organizations, people, and events
CCIR	commander's critical information requirement
COA	course of action
COS	chief of staff
DA	Department of the Army
DS	direct support
EEFI	essential element of friendly information
FFIR	friendly force information requirement
FM	field manual
GS	general support
GSR	general support-reinforcing
IPB	intelligence preparation of the battlefield
JP	joint publication
ISR	intelligence, surveillance, and reconnaissance
MDMP	military decisionmaking process
METT-TC	mission, enemy, terrain and weather, troops and support available, time available, and civil considerations
MOE	measure of effectiveness
MOP	measure of performance
OPCON	operational control
OPLAN	operation plan
OPORD	operation order
ORSA	operations research/systems analyst
PIR	priority intelligence requirement
PMESII-PT	political, military, economic, social, information, infrastructure, physical environment, and time
R	reinforcing
RDSP	rapid decisionmaking and syncronization process
SOP	standard operating procedure

TACON	tactical control
TLP	troop leading procedures
U.S.	United States
WARNO	warning order
XO	executive officer

SECTION II – TERMS

administrative control

Direction or exercise of authority over subordinate or other organizations in respect to administration and support, including organization of Service forces, control of resources and equipment, personnel management, unit logistics, individual and unit training, readiness, mobilization, demobilization, discipline, and other matters not included in the operational missions of the subordinate or other organizations. (JP 1)

airspace control

A process used to increase operational effectiveness by promoting the safe, efficient, and flexible use of airspace. (JP 3-52)

Army design methodology

A methodology for applying critical and creative thinking to understand, visualize, and describe problems and approaches to solving them. (ADP 5-0)

assessment

Determination of the progress toward accomplishing a task, creating a condition, or achieving an objective. (JP 3-0)

assign

(Joint) To place units or personnel in an organization where such placement is relatively permanent, and/or where such organization controls and administers the unitsor personnel for the primary function, or greater portion of the functions, of the unit or personnel. (JP 3-0)

attach

(Joint) The placement of units or personnel in an organization where such placement is relatively temporary. (JP 3-0)

battle rhythm

(Joint) A deliberate daily cycle of command, staff, and unit activities intended to synchronize current and future operations. (JP 3-33)

*civil considerations

The influence of manmade infrastructure, civilian institutions, and activities of the civilian leaders, populations, and organizations within an area of operations on the conduct of military operations.

*collaborative planning

Commanders, subordinate commanders, staffs, and other partners sharing information, knowledge, perceptions, ideas, and concepts regardless of physical location throughout the planning process.

commander's critical information requirement

An information requirement identified by the commander as being critical to facilitating timely decisionmaking. (JP 3-0)

commander's intent

A clear and concise expression of the purpose of the operation and the desired military end state that supports mission command, provides focus to the staff, and helps subordinate and supporting commanders act to achieve the commander's desired results without further orders, even when the operation does not unfold as planned. (JP 3-0)

commander's visualization

The mental process of developing situational understanding, determining a desired end state, and envisioning an operational approach by which the force will achieve that end state. (ADP 5-0)

*concept of operations

(Army) A statement that directs the manner in which subordinate units cooperate to accomplish the mission and establishes the sequence of actions the force will use to achieve the end state.

*confirmation brief

A briefing subordinate leaders give to the higher commander immediately after the operation order is given. It is the leaders' understanding of the commander's intent, their specific tasks, and the relationship between their mission and the other units in the operation.

control measure

A means of regulating forces or warfighting functions. (ADRP 6-0)

decision point

(Joint) A point in space and time when the commander or staff anticipates making a key decision concerning a specific course of action. (JP 5-0)

*decision support matrix

A written record of a war-gamed course of action that describes decision points and associated actions at those decision points.

decision support template

A combined intelligence and operations graphic based on the results of wargaming. The decision support template depicts decision points, timelines associated with movement of forces and the flow of the operation, and other key items of information required to execute a specific friendly course of action. (JP 2-01.3)

decisive point

A geographic place, specific key event, critical factor, or function that, when acted upon, allows commanders to gain a marked advantage over an adversary or contribute materially to achieving success. (JP 3-0)

*direct support

(Army) A support relationship requiring a force to support another specific force and authorizing it to answer directly to the supported force's request for assistance.

*essential element of friendly information

(Army) A critical aspect of a friendly operation that, if known by the enemy, would subsequently compromise, lead to failure, or limit success of the operation and therefore should be protected from enemy detection.

*evaluating

Using criteria to judge progress toward desired conditions and determining why the current degree of progress exists.

execution

Putting a plan into action by applying combat power to accomplish the mission. (ADP 5-0)

*execution matrix

A visual and sequential representation of the critical tasks and responsible organizations by time.

friendly force information requirement

(Joint) Information the commander and staff need to understand the status of friendly force and supporting capabilities. (JP 3-0)

general support

That support which is given to the supported force as a whole and not to any particular subdivision thereof. (JP 3-09.3)

*general support-reinforcing

(Army) A support relationship assigned to a unit to support the force as a whole and to reinforce another similar-type unit.

graphic control measure

A symbol used on maps and displays to regulate forces and warfighting functions. (ADRP 6-0)

*indicator

(Army) In the context of assessment, an item of information that provides insight into a measure of effectiveness or measure of performance.

information collection

An activity that synchronizes and integrates the planning and employment of sensors and assets as well as the processing, exploitation, and dissemination of systems in direct support of current and future operations. (FM 3-55)

liaison

That contact or intercommunication maintained between elements of military forces or other agencies to ensure mutual understanding and unity of purpose and action. (JP 3-08)

*key tasks

Those activities the force must perform as a whole to achieve the desired end state.

line of effort

(Army) A line that links multiple tasks using the logic of purpose rather than geographical reference to focus efforts toward establishing operational and strategic conditions. (ADRP 3-0)

line of operations

(Army) A line that defines the directional orientation of a force in time and space in relation to the enemy and that links the force with its base of operations and objectives. (ADRP 3-0)

main effort

A designated subordinate unit whose mission at a given point in time is most critical to overall mission success. (ADRP 3-0)

measure of effectiveness

A criterion used to assess changes in system behavior, capability, or operational environment that is tied to measuring the attainment of an end state, achievement of an objective, or creation of an effect. (JP 3-0)

measure of performance

A criterion used to assess friendly actions that is tied to measuring task accomplishment. (JP 3-0)

military decisionmaking process

An iterative planning methodology to understand the situation and mission, develop a course of action, and produce an operation plan or order. (ADP 5-0)

mission

The task, together with the purpose, that clearly indicates the action to be taken and the reason therefore. (JP 3-0)

mission command

(Army) The exercise of authority and direction by the commander using mission orders to enable disciplined initiative within the commander's intent to empower agile and adaptive leaders in the conduct of unified land operations. (ADP 6-0)

mission command warfighting function

The related tasks and systems that develop and integrate those activities enabling a commander to balance the art of command and the science of control in order to integrate the other warfighting functions. (ADRP 3-0)

mission orders

Directives that emphasize to subordinates the results to be attained, not how they are to achieve them. (ADP 6-0)

*monitoring

Continuous observation of those conditions relevant to the current operation.

*nested concepts

A planning technique to achieve unity of purpose whereby each succeeding echelon's concept of operations is aligned by purpose with the higher echelons' concept of operations.

objective

1. (Joint) The clearly defined, decisive, and attainable goal toward which every operation is directed. (JP 5-0) 2. (Army) a location on the ground used to orient operations, phase operations, facilitate changes of direction, and provide for unity of effort. (FM 3-90)

operational approach

A description of the broad actions the force must take to transform current conditions into those desired at end state. (JP 5-0)

operational art

The cognitive approach by commanders and staffs — supported by their skill, knowledge, experience, creativity, and judgment — to develop strategies, campaigns, and operations to organize and employ military forces by integrating ends, ways, and means. (JP 3-0)

operational control

A command authority that may be exercised by commanders at any echelon at or below the level of combatant command. Operational control is inherent in combatant command (command authority) and may be delegated within the command. Operational control is the authority to perform those functions of command over subordinate forces involving organizing and employing commands and forces, assigning tasks, designating objectives, and giving authoritative direction necessary to accomplish the mission. Operational control includes authoritative direction over all aspects of military operations and joint training necessary to accomplish missions assigned to the command. Operational control should be exercised through the commanders of subordinate organizations. Normally this authority is exercised through subordinate joint force commanders and Service and/or functional component commanders. Operational control normally provides full authority to organize commands and forces and to employ those forces as the commander in operational control considers necessary to accomplish assigned missions; it does not, in and of itself, include authoritative direction for logistics or matters of administration, discipline, internal organization, or unit training. (JP 3-0)

operations process

The major mission command activities performed during operations: planning, preparing, executing, and continuously assessing the operation. (ADP 5-0)

organic

Assigned to and forming an essential part of a military organization. Organic parts of a unit are those listed in its table of organization for the Army, Air Force, and Marine Corps, and are assigned to the administrative organizations of the operating forces for the Navy. (JP 1-02)

*parallel planning

Is two or more echelons planning for the same operation sharing information sequentially through warning orders from the higher headqarters prior to the headquarters publishing their operation plan or operation order.

phase

(Army) A planning and execution tool used to divide an operation in duration or activity. (ADRP 3-0)

planning

The art and science of understanding a situation, envisioning a desired future, and laying out effective ways of bringing that future about. (ADP 5-0)

*planning horizon

A point in time commanders use to focus the organization's planning efforts to shape future events.

preparation

Those activities performed by units and Soldiers to improve their ability to execute an operation. (ADP 5-0)

priority intelligence requirement

(Joint) An intelligence requirement, stated as a priority for intelligence support, that the commander and staff need to understand the adversary or the operational environment. (JP 2-0)

protection

The preservation of the effectiveness and survivability of mission-related military and nonmilitary personnel, equipment, facilities, information, and infrastructure deployed or located within or outside the boundaries of a given operational area. (JP 3-0)

*priority of support

A priority set by the commander to ensure a subordinate unit has support in accordance with its relative importance to accomplish the mission.

prudent risk

A deliberate exposure to potential injury or loss when the commander judges the outcome in terms of mission accomplishment as worth the cost. (ADP 6-0)

*rehearsal

A session in which a staff or unit practices expected actions to improve performance during execution.

*reinforcing

A support relationship requiring a force to support another supporting unit.

risk management

The process of identifying, assessing, and controlling risks arising from operational factors and making decisions that balance risk cost with mission benefits. (JP 3-0)

running estimate

The continuous assessment of the current situation used to determine if the current operation is proceeding according to the commander's intent and if planned future operations are supportable. (ADP 5-0)

security operations

Security operations are those operations undertaken by a commander to provide early and accurate warning of enemy operations, to provide the force being protected with time and maneuver space within which to react to the enemy, and to develop the situation to allow the commander to effectively use the protected force. (FM 3-90)

situational understanding

The product of applying analysis and judgment to relevant information to determine the relationships among the operational and mission variables to facilitate decisionmaking. (ADP 5-0)

tactical control

Command authority over assigned or attached forces or commands, or military capability or forces made available for tasking, that is limited to the detailed direction and control of movements or maneuvers within the operational area necessary to accomplish missions or tasks assigned. Tactical control is inherent in operational control. Tactical control may be delegated to, and exercised at any level at or below the level of combatant command. Tactical control provides sufficient authority for controlling and directing the application of force or tactical use of combat support assets within the assigned mission or task. (JP 3-0)

targeting

The process of selecting and prioritizing targets and matching the appropriate response to them, considering operational requirements and capabilities. (JP 3-0)

*task organization

(Army) A temporary grouping of forces designed to accomplish a particular mission.

task-organizing

The act of designing an operating force, support staff, or sustainment package of specific size and composition to meet a unique task or mission. (ADRP 3-0)

*terrain management

The process of allocating terrain by establishing areas of operation, designating assembly areas, and specifying locations for units and activities to deconflict activities that might interfere with each other.

troop leading procedures

A dynamic process used by small-unit leaders to analyze a mission, develop a plan, and prepare for an operation. (ADP 5-0)

unified action partners

Those military forces, governmental and nongovernmental organizations, and elements of the private sector with whom Army forces plan, coordinate, synchronize, and integrate during the conduct of operations. (ADRP 3-0)

References

Field manuals and selected joint publications are listed by new number followed by old number.

REQUIRED PUBLICATIONS

These documents must be available to intended users of this publication.

FM 1-02 (101-5-1). *Operational Terms and Graphics*. 21 September 2004.

JP 1-02. *Department of Defense Dictionary of Military and Associated Terms*. 8 November 2010.

RELATED PUBLICATIONS

These documents contain relevant supplemental information.

JOINT PUBLICATIONS

Most joint publications are available online: <http://www.dtic.mil/doctrine/new_pubs/jointpub htm.>

JP 1. *Doctrine for the Armed Forces of the United States*. 2 May 2007.

JP 2-0. *Joint Intelligence*. 22 June 2007.

JP 2-01. *Joint and National Intelligence Support to Military Operations*. 5 January 2012.

JP 2-01.3. *Joint Intelligence Preparation of the Operational Environment*. 16 June 2009.

JP 3-0. *Joint Operations*. 11 August 2011.

JP 3-08. *Interorganizational Coordination During Joint Operations*. 24 June 2011.

JP 3-09.3. *Close Air Support*. 8 July 2009.

JP 3-33. *Joint Task Force Headquarters*. 16 February 2007.

JP 3-52. *Joint Airspace Control*. 20 May 2010.

JP 5-0. *Joint Operation Planning*. 11 August 2011.

ARMY PUBLICATIONS

Most Army doctrinal publications are available online: <http://www.apd.army.mil/>.

ADP 3-0 (FM 3-0). *Unified Land Operations*. 10 October 2011.

ADP 5-0 (FM 5-0). *The Operations Process*. 17 May 2012.

ADP 6-0 (FM 6-0). *Mission Command*. 17 May 2012.

ADRP 3-0. *Unified Land Operations*. 16 May 2012.

ADRP 6-0. *Mission Command*. 17 May 2012.

ATTP 2-01. *Planning Requirements and Assessing Collection*. 23 April 2012.

ATTP 5-0.1. *Commander and Staff Officer Guide*. 14 September 2011.

FM 3-55. *Information Collection*. 23 April 2012.

FM 3-90. *Tactics*. 4 July 2001.

FM 27-10. *The Law of Land Warfare*. 18 July 1956.

SOURCE USED

This source is quoted in this publication.

Eisenhower, Dwight D. "Remarks at the National Defense Executive Reserve Conference."

14 November 1957, edited by John T. Woolley and Gerhard Peters, *The American Presidency Project* [online]. Santa Barbara, CA. Available from World Wide Web:

<http://www.presidency.ucsb.edu/ws/?pid=10951> (accessed 12 January 2012).

PRESCRIBED FORMS

None

REFERENCED FORMS

DA Form 2028. *Recommended Changes to Publications and Blank Forms.*

Index

Entries are by paragraph number unless specified otherwise.

A

accept prudent risk to exploit opportunities, 4-6–4-10

activities of the Army design methodology, 2-30–2-51

administrative control, 2-82

airspace control, 1-63–1-64

anticipate events and adapt to changing circumstances, 2-11–2-13

apply critical and creative thinking, 1-40–1-42

Army command relationships, 2-75–2-84

Army design methodology, 2-24–2-29
  activities of the, 2-30–2-51
  and the military decisionmaking process, 2-61–2-63
  defined, 2-24

Army planning methodologies, 2-23–2-68

Army support relationships, 2-85–2-90

assess, 1-30

assessment, 5-1–5-35
  and decisionmaking, 4-25
  and the operations process, 5-1–5-2
  defined, 5-1
  guides to effective, 5-22–5-26
  process, 5-3–5-21
  support, 5-32–5-35
  working groups, 5-27–5-31

assign, defined, 2-78

attach, defined, 2-79

B-C

battle rhythm, 1-65–1-68
  defined, 1-65

build and maintain situational understanding, 1-31

civil considerations, defined, 1-35

collaborative planning, defined, 2-125

combine quantitative and qualitative indicators, 5-26

command sergeants major, 4-14

commander's critical information requirements, 1-22–1-26
  defined, 1-22

commander's intent, 1-18–1-19, 2-92–2-96

commanders, 4-12

commanders drive the operations process, 1-11–1-46

commanders focus planning, 2-120

commanders prioritize the assessment effort, 5-23

compare the current situation to the order, 4-36–4-37

complete, task organization, 3-22

concept of operations, 2-97–2-98
  defined, 2-97

conduct, confirmation briefs, 3-16
  plans-to-operations transition, 3-18–3-20
  preoperations checks and inspections, 3-25
  rehearsals, 3-17

confirmation brief, defined, 3-16

confirmation briefs, conduct, 3-16

continuing activities, 1-47, 1-57–1-64

control measure, defined, 2-114

control measures, 2-114–2-118

coordinating and conducting liaison, 3-3–3-5

coordinating instructions, 2-113

cultural understanding, 1-36–1-39

current state, of an operational environment, 2-35–2-37

D

decision point, defined, 4-23

decision support matrix, defined, 4-20

decision support template, defined, 4-20

decisionmaking, and assessment, 4-25
  during execution, 4-22–4-24

decisive point, defined, 2-102

decisive points and objections, 2-102–2-104

deputy commanders, 4-13

describe, 1-17

desired end state of an operational environment, 2-38–2-40

determine the type of decision required, 4-39–4-40

develop, a course of action, 4-41–4-45
  an operational approach, 2-44–2-46
  simple, flexible plans through mission orders, 2-121–2-123

direct, 1-28

direct support, defined, 2-87

document results, 2-47–2-48

E

effective planning, guides to, 2-119–2-127

effectiveness, measure of, 5-11

encourage collaboration and dialogue, 1-43–1-46

ensure forces and resources are ready and positioned, 3-31

essential elements of friendly information, 1-27

evaluating, 5-9–5-17
  defined, 5-9

execution, 4-1–4-51
  decisionmaking during, defined, 4-1
  fundamentals of, 4-1–4-3
  responsibilities during, 4-11

execution matrix, defined, 4-21

F

frame an operational environment, 2-33

frame the problem, 2-41–2-43

framing, 2-25–2-26

friendly force requirement, 1-26

fundamentals of, execution, 4-1–4-3,
  the operations process, 1-1–1-72

G

general support, defined, 2-88

general support-reinforcing, 2-90

Entries are by paragraph number unless specified otherwise.

Entries are by paragraph number unless specified otherwise.

By order of the Secretary of the Army:

RAYMOND T. ODIERNO
General, United States Army
Chief of Staff

Official:

JOYCE E. MORROW
Administrative Assistant to the
Secretary of the Army
1211502

DISTRIBUTION:

Active Army, Army National Guard, and United States Army Reserve: To be distributed in accordance with the initial distribution number (IDN) 110412, requirements for ADRP 5-0.

Made in the USA
Lexington, KY
28 November 2016